T0171676

To Hell with Culture

'Part of today's ideological debate . . . He lends insight to any number of topics, for instance patronage, success, the revolutionary nature of the arts.'

New York Times Book Review

'One of the foremost English intellectuals of this century.'

James King

'Read must be accounted as one of the most interesting and penetrating minds of our time . . . his work has actually modified the thought and practice of our age.'

Francis Berry

Herbert
Read

To Hell with Culture

And other essays on art and society

With a new introduction by Michael Paraskos

 London and New York

First published 1963
by Routledge & Kegan Paul

First published in Routledge Classics 2002
by Routledge
2 Park Square, Milton Park, Abingdon, Oxon OX14 4RN
711 Third Avenue, New York, NY 10017 (8th floor)

Routledge is an imprint of the Taylor & Francis Group, an informa business

© 1963 The Herbert Read Trust
Introduction to the Routledge Classics edition © 2002 Michael Paraskos

Typeset in Joanna by RefineCatch Limited, Bungay, Suffolk

British Library Cataloguing in Publication Data
A catalogue record for this book is available from the British Library

Library of Congress Cataloging in Publication Data
A catalog record for this book has been requested

ISBN 13: 978-0-415-28992-4 (hbk)
ISBN 13: 978-0-415-28993-1 (pbk)

To the Memory of
Eric Gill
1882–1940

CONTENTS

INTRODUCTION TO THE ROUTLEDGE CLASSICS EDITION

The decision of Routledge to reissue Herbert Read's seminal text *To Hell with Culture and Other Essays* is only the latest part of a revival of interest in this Modernist critic that has taken place over the last decade. The process can be seen to have begun with the major exhibition, held in England at Leeds City Art Galleries, in 1993, entitled *Herbert Read: A British Vision of World Art*, in which artworks by diverse artists, ranging from little-known figures such as Jacob Kramer and Bruce Turner to international Modernists such as Pablo Picasso and Henry Moore, were used to contextualize Read as one of the major critics and theorists of Modernism of the twentieth century.[1] Since then a slow but steady progression of Read-related texts has appeared, including both the republication of his writings and new critical analysis.[2]

---

[1] Benedict Read and David Thistlewood (eds), *Herbert Read: A British Vision of World Art* (London, Lund Humphries), 1993.

[2] For example, *Herbert Read, A One Man Manifesto* (London, Freedom Press), 1994, and David Goodway (ed.), *Herbert Read Reassessed* (Liverpool, Liverpool University Press), 1998.

Despite this recent development, the degree of neglect afforded to Read since his death in 1968 has been remarkable. Very quickly his ideas fell from view and other forms of criticism took over which responded, quite legitimately, to new forms of visual culture for which Read's ideas were, perhaps, inappropriate. Indeed, despite a reputation as a tireless supporter of 'the new' in art, towards the end of his life Read became disillusioned with what he saw as the increasing trivialisation of contemporary art, and he was particularly dismayed by the rise of Pop Art,[3] a movement whose legacy has been one of the dominating influences on the art world for the last quarter of a century. Yet there is both anecdotal and documented evidence to suggest a more disturbing reason for Read's disappearance from the critical landscape. This indicates that some anti-Readian critics and historians used his death as an opportunity to take revenge on the man once dubbed 'the Pope of Modern Art', and formulate a revisionist history that actively wrote out Read's contribution to the understanding of Modernism.[4]

At this point, perhaps, it is worth noting the reason for my own escape from this mainstream response to Read. Before I entered university in 1989, Read had been a sort of folk hero in my family as a result of the arrest of my father, the artist Stass Paraskos, in 1966 on a charge of exhibiting 'obscene' paintings at an exhibition at the Institute Gallery, in Leeds.[5] The objection to these artworks stemmed from their depiction of full-frontal male nudes, although it seems bizarre today that they were ever deemed pornographic, being painted in a highly non-

---

[3] Herbert Read, 'The disintegration of form in modern art', reproduced in Herbert Read, *The Origins of Form in Art* (London, Thames and Hudson), 1965, pp. 175–6.

[4] See Jerald Zaslove, 'Herbert Read and essential modernism', in Goodway, op. cit., p. 293.

[5] Alan Travis, *Bound and Gagged* (London, Profile Books), 2000, p. 202.

naturalistic style. My father, an immigrant from the British colony of Cyprus, was extremely frightened at his arrest, but Herbert Read came in, told him not to worry and even offered to pay for the services of the solicitor John Mortimer, who later became a popular novelist. Read also spoke at the ensuing trial, despite the fact he was extremely ill with cancer at the time,[6] and all of these experiences became part of my family history. Consequently, when I later became a young art history student I questioned the often automatic assumption of many of my tutors that Read was not worth reading.[7] Indeed it would be difficult to over-estimate the strength of such assumptions, and wrong to believe they have entirely gone away as Read is still routinely excluded from a number of key academic texts on art and literary history where his presence ought to be expected.

There are several possible explanations as to why Read was (and is) often excluded from critical histories, but the most convincing stems from the increasing dominance of Marxist forms of criticism from the 1970s onwards which, particularly in Read's birthplace, England, but also North America,[8] left him with an implacably hostile audience. In fact one of the leading theorists and practitioners of Marxist criticism during this time, Raymond Williams, seemed to confirm this by admitting that when he wrote his influential text *Culture and Society*, and effectively established a Marxist 'canon' for the practice of modern cultural studies,[9] he gladly excluded Read to whom he was 'implacably hostile'.[10] The legacy of this has been that those who followed on from Williams and used his Marxist methodology

---

[6] Stass Paraskos, *Homage to Herbert Read*, exhibition catalogue (Canterbury, Canterbury College of Art), 1984, p. 42.

[7] An honourable exception was Dr Tom Steele, author of the book *Alfred Orage and the Leeds Arts Club* (Aldershot, Scolar Press), 1990.

[8] See Jonathan Harris, *The New Art History* (London, Routledge), 2001, pp. 1–28.

[9] Zaslove, op. cit. pp. 301–3.

[10] Raymond Williams, *Politics and Letters* (London, New Left Books), 1979, p. 99.

as a foundation for their own work, such as Terry Eagleton, have perpetuated the absence of Read.

Yet, paradoxically, Read's criticism had a number of features in common with Marxism, even parallelling, while pre-dating, to some extent the work of Williams,[11] and nowhere was this more apparent than in *To Hell with Culture*. For example, in the preface Read stated explicitly that he accepted the basic Marxist proposition that social conditions shape the form, reception and use of artworks,[12] while in essays such as 'The Symptoms of Decadence' and 'The Collective Patron' he showed himself to be concerned with precisely the types of question that exercised the minds of Marxist critics, between the 1930s and 1970s, agreeing with them that in Capitalist societies patrons only supported those arts over which they could maintain some economic, and therefore political, control.[13] Although Karl Marx had himself been uncertain as to whether such a materialist social paradigm could be fully applied to the arts, very early on neo-Marxists formulated it into a theory that the arts were a product of the social conditions in which they were made, and subsequent appreciation of them was the product of the social context in which they were viewed.[14] An example of this was Arnold Hauser, who took the basic dialectical theory of Marxism, in which society was seen in terms of the opposition of the bourgeoisie and the proletariat, and correlated it to the various hierarchies, such as high and low art, art and craft, history and genre painting, and so on, that existed in the arts.[15] This suggested that the arts were created, used and manipulated by socially-dominant groups in order to maintain their positions of

[11] Zaslove, op. cit. p. 302.

[12] Herbert Read, *To Hell with Culture* (London, Routledge), 1963, p. x.

[13] Ibid., pp. 88–90.

[14] Donald Drew Egbert, *Social Radicalism and the Arts* (New York, Alfred A. Knopf), 1970, p. 86f.

[15] Arnold Hauser, *The Philosophy of Art History* (London, Routledge), 1959, p. 279f.

power, and the arts came to be seen as a socially conservative force designed to maintain the iniquitous economic and political status quo,[16] all of which Read, with some modifications we shall see, was willing to accept. In fact, Read was prominent in promoting the ideas of a number of Marxist critics in his role as a director of the publishing house Routledge, including Hauser.[17]

There were, however, also fundamental differences between Read and the neo-Marxists, and these stemmed largely from his insistence that a firm distinction needed to be made between art and culture. This was necessary, Read stated in the preface of *To Hell with Culture*, to address questions as to the nature and origin of art, and its aesthetic value, which Marxist critics generally ignored and arguably were incapable of answering.[18] Thus, Read deviated from Marxism by suggesting that what it described as the social function of art, was in reality the function of culture, whilst the term 'art' should be reserved for processes that are far more fundamental, and linked to the very biology of the human body. The measure of this deviation can perhaps be gauged by comparing standard Marxist views on the body with those of Read. Marxist theorists tended to hold that the biological reality of the body was largely irrelevant to society or culture, and treated it as little more than an 'empty box', that is born without character or personality, and as something that was only formed into a character and personality by the society in which it is socialized.[19] Read, however, rejected this and shortly after the First World War used aspects of the new science of psychoanalysis to reinstate the body as a key element in human existence. In doing so he latched on to the ideas of a number of

[16] Ibid., p. 30.
[17] Egbert, op. cit. pp. 564–7.
[18] Read, *To Hell with Culture*, p. 30.
[19] Egbert, op. cit. pp. 86–7.

psychoanalysts who argued that individual and social motivation was rooted not in the power relationships of contemporary society, but in the unconscious needs or desires of the body, with the most well-known of these motivating desires being Sigmund Freud's theory of the libido.[20] The force of the libido, Freud had argued, was so great that it was an unavoidable necessity for the body to release it, but that this was frequently prevented by the higher levels of the mind due to the potential of the libido to disrupt ordered social life. Indeed, even without social factors, the mind was forced into this act of repression by the nature of the libido, which often comprised contradictory and incompatible desires in itself. Consequently the libido was repressed, and through this repression became distorted, or 'sublimated', into other forms through which it could be released. Sometimes this release might seem innocuous, such as with libidinous sexual attraction being expressed 'accidentally' through a slip of the tongue or an unintended pun; but it could also take an extreme form in neurotic and psychotic behaviour. However, as George Whitehead noted in his 1930 book *Psychoanalysis and Art*, of which Read possessed a copy,[21] Freud held the view that art was also a product of the sublimated libido. Whitehead wrote: 'With regard to art and culture we need a certain amount of undischarged (i.e. repressed) libido for the purpose of sublimation. Otherwise, there is no motive power available for creative energy.'[22] This allowed Read to argue that the need to make art arose from the needs or desires of the human body.[23]

Inevitably, this rooting of creativity in human biology placed greater emphasis on the role of the individual in making art than

[20] Herbert Read, 'Psychoanalysis and the Critic', *The Criterion*, vol. 3, no. 10, 1925, pp. 216–20.

[21] Now in the Herbert Read Archive, Brotherton Library, University of Leeds.

[22] George Whitehead, *Psychoanalysis and Art* (London, Faber), 1930, p. 13.

[23] Read, *To Hell with Culture*, p. 78.

those theories that lay greater stress on art as a social phenomenon. In the political climate of the 1930s and 40s this led Read
to ally himself with political anarchism,[24] in which human
individualism was also stressed, in opposition to the collectivism of Marxism and fascism. Consequently, it might be possible
to argue that the neglect of Read by later Marxist historians
had its origin in this early political difference. Indeed, it is
tempting to compare it to the uneasy relationship that existed
between the Marxists and anarchists in the Spanish Civil War at
precisely this time. Although both anarchists and Marxists
fought against the fascist forces of Francisco Franco, they were
also often ideologically and physically hostile to each other,[25] as
shown by the notorious and bloody suppression of anarchists
in Barcelona by Marxist troops in May 1937. The comparison is
particularly apposite given the public argument Read had in
1938 with the then Marxist art historian Anthony Blunt over
Picasso's painting Guernica, which depicted the bombing in
1937 of the Spanish Basque town of the same name by pro-
fascist German forces. Blunt attacked the picture for failing to
realize 'the political significance of Guernica',[26] but Read ridi-
culed Blunt for suggesting that Picasso should have painted an
image that appealed solely to the ideological beliefs of 'the
communist in his cell'. Guernica was instead a quasi-religious
picture, Read suggested, showing the agony of humanity under
the bombing.[27]

In a very real sense To Hell with Culture was a continuation of
Read's attacks of the 1930s on Marxist political and, more especially, cultural theories, as well as his proposition of a viable
radical alternative. Many of the essays included in the volume do

[24] Herbert Read, *Anarchy and Order* (London, Faber), 1954, pp. 44–8.

[25] Ibid., pp. 89–90.

[26] Cited in Robert Radford, *Art for a Purpose: The Artists' International Association*
(Winchester, Winchester School of Art Press), 1987, p. 90.

[27] Herbert Read, 'Picasso's Guernica', in *London Bulletin*, October 1938, p. 6.

in fact date from this period, and had been previously published by Routledge under the title *The Politics of the Unpolitical and Other Essays*.[28] Yet, as shown by the essay entitled 'The Politics of the Unpolitical', which remained in *To Hell with Culture*, Read believed he was attacking more fundamental principles than simply the political label 'Marxism', and to be fair to Marxism he was equally scathing of its fascistic and democratic rivals.[29] This linked his work very closely to that of his friend George Orwell, and it would be very easy to read many of the essays in *To Hell with Culture* as the political tract equivalents to Orwell's novels, *Animal Farm* and *Nineteen Eighty-Four*. In both writers there were parallel fears that all ideology, whether from the political left, right or centre, led inevitably to the same dehumanized form of society. Instead of this, Read aimed to suggest another way, an 'unpolitical politics', by which he meant social life conducted without an individual having to submit him or her self to social conformity or external ideology. In fact, in 'The Freedom of the Artist', Read indicated that such a society was the ideal utopia to which he strove,[30] and one might argue that this was also the type of life dreamed of by Winston Smith, the hapless hero of Orwell's *Nineteen Eighty-Four*, before his discovery that such a life is nigh impossible in a world where those who are ideologically driven will enforce their views on others, often in violent ways. For Read, Marxism sought to do nothing more than replace the dogma of bourgeois culture with the equally pernicious dogma of a proletarian culture, all of which he, like Orwell, saw as little different in substance to the dogma of fascism.[31]

This divergence from Marxism was also evident in the essays

[28] Herbert Read, *The Politics of the Unpolitical and Other Essays* (London, Routledge), 1945.

[29] Read, *To Hell with Culture*, pp. 38–48.

[30] Ibid., pp. 117–18.

[31] Ibid., p. 41.

'The Symptoms of Decadence' and 'The Collective Patron', where Read attacked the economic and political control of the bourgeoisie over the arts in a decidedly moral tone that had more in common with several nineteenth-century critics he admired, such as John Ruskin and William Morris, than later Marxism. In exercising control, Read argued, 'Vanity in the patron of art leads to servitude in the artist', and that a 'servile mind is a mind that has committed moral suicide'. Equally Ruskinian is the sense of moral authority with which Read felt able to make such sweeping condemnations of the history of art as 'there is scarcely a great artist in the history of modern civilization whose work would not have been incomparably greater if he could have lived in spiritual and economic security'.[32] When one reads such phrases as 'spiritual security', it is not difficult to conclude that one is not reading a Marxist tract.

Similarly, if 'The Symptoms of Decadence' can be described as an essay in which Read outlined problems that Marxists saw as outside their remit, in 'The Collective Patron' he sought to suggest concrete, but equally non-Marxist, solutions. For an artist to thrive, he argued, they needed three things—appreciation, patronage and liberty. The first of these reflected Read's belief that the artist had a social function that required that he or she engaged with society, and vice versa, as can be seen in his statement that, 'The essential thing is for the artist to have the sense of an audience: to feel that his voice is not echoing in an empty room, with no response'. On patronage, Read suggested,

It is a fact of no small significance that a great majority of the painters, poets and composers who have risen to fame since the disappearance of the (seventeenth-century) patronage system have been men with independent incomes derived from inherited estates'.

[32] Ibid., pp. 88–90.

This had been sufficient to immunize them from the effects of Capitalistic and other forms of servile patronage, but for artists without private incomes there needed to be some other form of support that had the same effect. This led on to Read's third requirement, liberty. He wrote, 'Patronage of some kind is essential, but it is only tolerable when accompanied by liberty'.[33]

In trying to formulate positive suggestions, Read's was to some extent indebted to the ideas of his friend, the sculptor Eric Gill, to whom *To Hell with Culture* was dedicated. Artists might, Read wrote, form something like a co-operative guild, analogous to a Mediaeval crafts guild, which would give them enough corporate strength to protect themselves from patron interference and ensure an equitable distribution of common wealth.[34] Again, such views had nineteenth-century antecedents, including Ruskin's Guild of St. George, and it is not too much of an exaggeration to see Read as a very late Gothic Revivalist, even if he had, rather like the 'Gothic Revivalists' who formed the German Bauhaus, a Modernist edge. Read had, of course, already published a pamphlet, in 1935, entitled *Essential Communism*, in which he suggested what was effectively a co-operative 'guild-ism' as an alternative to Marxist collectivism.[35] Nonetheless, as he recognised in 'The Collective Patron' the problem with promoting such ideas was that the closest available equivalents that he could hold up as examples were, ironically, the Marxist artists' co-operatives in the Soviet Union. In these, Read acknowledged, artists were still subject to some of the worst forms of censorship and the patron individual had been merely replaced by the Patron State.[36]

[33] Ibid., p. 94f.

[34] Ibid., pp. 95–6.

[35] Herbert Read, *Essential Communism* (London, Stanley Nott Ltd), 1935.

[36] Read, *To Hell with Culture*, pp. 96–7.

Yet, running through 'The Collective Patron' were hints, indicated by just a few scattered sentences, that Read was not really an advocate of 'co-operative guilds' in any case. He had long had an ambiguous attitude towards the Guild Movement, which it is worth remembering was a serious and relatively powerful political force in the early twentieth century,[37] and it was not as a guildsman but a political anarchist that he admitted his true beliefs; 'The true solution of this problem, as I have insisted again and again in my writings, is the reintegration of art and work, so that art simply becomes the qualitative aspect of all that is made and done and said in a community'.[38] Such a solution would in fact make superfluous the idea of individual artists being responsible for art, and in so doing remove the pressure of vain and egotistical patrons on those individuals. It would in effect remove the 'profession' of artist completely.

As can be seen, Read rejected Marxism in a number of ways, but it was his adoption of Freudianism that was probably most significant. Nonetheless, early on he also came to reject the psychoanalytical theories of Freud, something that was not surprising since, at least as far as Read understood him, Freud had effectively suggested that artistic activity was little different to mental illness.[39] In Freud's place Read unified his long-standing interest in Idealist philosophy, and particularly the work of Friedrich von Schelling, Conrad Fiedler and Samuel Taylor Coleridge, with the theories of Freud's great rival in early psychoanalysis, Carl Gustav Jung.[40] Idealists tended to reject the idea that the body could know the physical world in which we

---

[37] For example, see Read's attitude to Arthur Penty, a leading promoter of the Guild Movement, as cited in James King, *The Last Modern* (London, Weidenfeld and Nicolson), 1990, p. 54.

[38] Read, *To Hell with Culture*, p. 98.

[39] For comment see John R. Doheny, 'Herbert Read's use of Sigmund Freud', in David Goodway (ed.), op. cit. pp. 74–9.

[40] Ibid.

live in an objective way, for the simple reason that it relied on the five subjective senses to provide it with information about that world. Instead, the body was seen to receive data from the senses and use this to construct a mental image, or possible version, of reality. Put more acurately, the unconscious was creating symbols for reality which it then re-presented to itself as reality. This form of Idealism was in fact influential on Jung, who similarly posited that a person's sense of reality was a product of the mind, and that consciousness resulted from the fusion of two distinct states. These states comprised the inner self (introversion) on one side, and the facility to engage with the outside world (extroversion) on the other. To Read it was a theory that suggested 'living reality is never the exclusive product of one or other of these contrasted attitudes, but only a specific vital activity which unites them (and) bridges the gulf between them'.[41] It was a non-Marxist dialectical theory that was to lie at the core of his writings more or less consistently throughout his life, despite claims from some critics that Read was an inconsistent theorist.

This is not to suggest, however, that Read saw the creation of works of art as a simple bi-product of the processes by which the body creates consciousness, any more than he believed that art was simply a product of the class war between the bourgeoisie and proletariat, or a form of sublimated libido.[42] On the contrary, he saw the physicality of art as being of the utmost importance as it was through the creation of physical objects that the symbols for reality generated by the mind were given any sense of longevity in human consciousness. Without this, a permanent sense of psychological anxiety or angst was likely, due to the constantly changing nature of reality.[43] However, this also

[41] Herbert Read, n. 20, pp. 216–20.

[42] Read, *To Hell with Culture*, p. 91.

[43] Herbert Read, *Icon and Idea* (London, Faber), 1955, p. 65.

explained historical change in art, since even a belief in the permanency of a symbol for reality was not the same as genuine permanency, no matter how fixed the symbol appeared to be in the form of an artwork, as the physical world of nature would eventually change to the point where the symbol of reality would no longer be viable. Thus, artists are needed to suggest continuously new symbols for reality that reflect such changes, an idea that implies that the history of art be seen as a history of the changing symbols for reality.

In *To Hell with Culture*, therefore, Read was suggesting that visual forms emerged from two sources. One of these was as a natural and biological response to the physical environment, and the other a cultural imposition. Read conceived this latter in terms very similar to those adopted by Marxist cultural theorists, with cultural values imposed on the mass of society by an economic-ally and politically dominant elite, who did so to suit their own ends and maintain their positions of power. Unlike Marxists, however, Read saw such positions of power as ultimately stemming from the social perception of reality, or conscious-ness, of a particular time and place. As artists challenged that perception of reality, and offered viable alternatives to it, the dominant position of the elite came under threat, and their response was always to try and shore up the old perceptions of reality that had given them their elevated positions in the first place. They thus created institutions to impose outdated and reified symbols for reality on the mass of the populace—such as national theatres, galleries and museums. Culture was, therefore, no more than dead art, cliché and the repetition of old symbols for reality, and its perseverance in society was both unhealthy and duplicitous.

There was perhaps nowhere that Read expressed his belief that cliche was the source of individual and social unhappiness and unhealthiness more clearly in *To Hell with Culture* than in the essay 'The Problem of Pornography'. In it, he argued that conflicting sexual or libidinous desires were an inevitable part of human psychology, but that societies handled them in different ways. In modern Western society the libido was repressed by cliché with the most common example being the repression of any memories from childhood of sexual desire. Thus people were lulled into a 'false memory' formed from the cliché of a sexless, innocent and happy childhood that they had not really experienced. Read also noted that even in adulthood open discussion of sexual desire was taboo, so that 'Sex becomes a dirty word'. Consequently, the libido is sublimated from its natural course in unhealthy ways, and 'all publication of sexual insubordination becomes that disreputable phenomenon ... pornography'. In other societies, however, such as pre-Europeanized Bali or fifth-century B.C. Athens, there was no pornography because there were no illusionary memories repressing real experience. The libido could thus be transformed into the symbols of art and myth and released in a socially acceptable form. 'The distinction', Read wrote,

> between art and illusion is a distinction between a lost experience that has been recovered and made part of the present reality, and a lost experience that remains unconscious because it is screened in cliches and the ready-made conventions of morality.[44]

In arguing that it was only the latter attitude to sex that led to pornography, and not sex, nudity or desire *per se*, it is easy to see why Read was much admired by Alex Comfort,[45] whose book *The Joy of Sex* did so much to launch the 'sexual revolution' of the

---

[44] Read, *To Hell with Culture*, p. 152f.
[45] Comfort dedicated his book *Art and Social Responsibility* (London, Falcon Press), 1946, to Read, and was involved with him in a number of projects. See John R. Doheny, 'Herbert Read as Literary Critic', in Goodway, op. cit. p. 62.

1960s and 70s. Also, it explains why Read was so supportive of my father at his trial in Leeds.[46]

To Hell with Culture is a collection of essays that displays Read's general libertarian attitude towards art and society, and intense ideological dislike of all forms of cultural control on the individual. In common with Marxist theorists, he saw bourgeois cultural institutions as deliberate agents for social control or, if founded with good intentions, too open to manipulation to be for the long term good. Unlike Marxists, however, his solution was not simply to replace those institutions with proletarian ones, but in accordance with his anarchist political beliefs, to empower individuals. As stated in 'A Civilization from Under', if institutions for art should exist they must not be places 'where the past is preserved', but experimental centres 'where the future is forecast'. Only in this way could they counter those reactionary forces that imposed on individuals their cultural values, and the iniquitous vision of reality that those cultural values represented. It was for this reason that Read stated, 'cultural institutions imposed on the masses are so much dead weight—to hell with such culture!'[47]

MICHAEL PARASKOS
Lecturer in Fine Art,
University of Hull
June 2002

---

[46] Benedict Read, 'Herbert Read: An Overview', in Benedict Read and David Thistlewood (eds), op. cit. pp. 18–20.

[47] Read, *To Hell with Culture*, p. 84.

PREFACE

Several of these essays are reprinted from a war-time volume which I called *The Politics of the Unpolitical*. By that paradoxical title I meant to indicate that the artist always has loyalties that transcend the political divisions of the society in which he lives. It was not an acceptable point of view in 1943, and after the war it seemed to be for ever superseded by various doctrines of *un art engagé*—an art dedicated to the defence and propagation of 'a way of life'—the way of life, in our Western world, being understood as free enterprise in economics and democratic forms of government. The fate of art and literature in countries where these values were denied, the totalitarian countries, was the proof by negation of art's involvement in the great political struggle of our time. It was not merely a question of maintaining our political liberty: culture itself—our poetry, our painting, our architecture and music—was threatened by our political opponents and had to be defended.

This defensive attitude was forced on the intellectuals of the West by the cultural aggression of the communists. The inexorable laws of Dialectical Materialism, we were told, applied not only to the economic structure of capitalism, but also to its idealistic superstructure. Both alike would perish and be replaced by a new society with its new cultural ideals. I need not refer to the many dialectical analyses of art and literature which traced their stylistic evolution in phases parallel to society's economic evolution.

In so far as culture is a superficial phenomenon (an epiphenomenon, as these sociologists call it), this materialistic interpretation is true; indeed, it does not require the methodology of Marxism to demonstrate that Homer's imagery springs from a neolithic culture, or Shakespeare's from a mercantile culture. Personally I can travel a long way with the Marxists in their analysis of the social origin of the forms and uses of art. What neither the Marxists nor their opponents can explain by their doctrinaire methods is the phenomenon of genius in art: they cannot explain the nature of the artist nor even the conditions that determine his eccentric existence.

In the history of art, the genius is finally all that matters. Unless Homer and Shakespeare and their kind had 'happened' in their inconsequent and unpredictable way, the history of art would be like the history of any other skill—tool-making or agriculture. Art is distinguished by its sudden glories, its irrational and irregular irruptions of light in the midst of a universal darkness.

It follows that art, in its essence, is independent of politics— as, indeed, it is independent of morals and all other temporal values. It is a sad and true fact that the artistic genius is ethically unreliable. The history of art is rife with perversion, adultery, covetousness and spite. In this respect artists are neither worse nor better than other men. As artists they are all too human.

The artist is the supreme egoist, and his fellow-citizens not only distrust him, but often would like to destroy him. In totalitarian societies this frequently happens, but even a bloody-minded tyrant like Stalin fears to eliminate a Pasternak. Pasternak is, indeed, the heroic prototype of the literary genius, incapable of conformity, fearless, identifying himself with humanity and not with a country, a political party or a doctrine. Genius always possesses this indefinite concreteness, this passionate particularity, this piecemeal integrity. It is of the essence of genius to be uncommitted to any abstraction.

By using the word 'genius' and by mentioning such prototypes as Homer and Shakespeare, Beethoven and Tolstoy, I may seem to be setting narrow limits to the field of art, but that is not my intention. Genius can be absolute, as we suppose it to have been in the case of Homer, but more frequently it is a rare visitation, a fire that seems to descend on the artist from another realm of being. There is nothing specifically aristocratic about it—it seems to be absolutely arbitrary in its manifestations, and can as likely visit the peasant's croft as the palace or academy. That is why it is illogical to associate it with political freedom. The artist enjoys freedom and is harassed by tyranny. But there is no reason to suppose that a democratic system of government, so-called, is any more favourable to the prevalence of art than the systems we call aristocratic, oligarchic or totalitarian.

I must make myself very clear, for this point of view is easily misrepresented, and yet is the central theme of my book.

There is, of course, a sense in which art is subject to the chances which beset any other form of life—it can simply be crushed by adverse physical forces, by war and famine and plague. In this respect art would suffer equally whatever the prevailing system of government. It can also suffer from neglect—genius can be stifled by poverty, ignorance and misunderstanding. But it is wrong to assume that there is any inherent force in democracy that encourages the emergence of the artist. Indeed, in so far as democracy is a levelling process—an ideology of normalcy and egality—it works against genius of any kind, and in particular against the individual whose work is not vendible by the usual economic methods. The artist is an 'outsider' in a democratic community, and all our schemes for democratic patronage of the arts cannot disguise the fact. Our present affluent societies cast a very wide net, but the meshes are coarse and the gesture is blind. It is in the nature of democracy that it cannot discriminate: its sensibility is blunted in committee work, dissipated in bureaucratic procedures, de-humanized by organizations. Aesthetic sensibility is indivisible: it is transmitted, as Martin Buber would say, only between man and man.

My conclusion, therefore, is that art in its creative aspects has little concern with democracy, or with communism,[1] or any other political system. It is an unpolitical manifestation of the human spirit, and though politicians may use it or abuse it for their ends, they can neither create it nor control it—nor destroy it.

This, however, does not mean that a society can ignore its artists. Indeed, my strongest belief is precisely the contrary. Art is always the index of social vitality, the moving finger that records the destiny of a civilization. A wise statesman should keep an anxious eye on this graph, for it is more significant than a decline in exports or a fall in the value of the nation's currency.

H. R.
OCTOBER, 1962

---

[1] On the ambiguity of these words, see pages 39–43 below.

AUTHOR'S NOTE

The essays collected in this volume are of various date and origin, and all have been submitted to a good deal of revision and rearrangement. The title essay was first published as a pamphlet in the Democratic Order Series (Routledge, 1941). This essay and nine others were collected in a volume entitled *The Politics of the Unpolitical* (Routledge 1943). To these I have now added five essays not hitherto published in a volume. Three of these first appeared in *The Sewanee Review, The London Magazine* and *The Saturday Review* (New York). The essay on pornography was contributed to a symposium on the subject published by Routledge & Kegan Paul (1961). 'The Secret of Success' was originally broadcast (in German) on the University of the Air. There are shorter passages incorporated from other sources. I would like to thank those editors who gave my opinions their first publicity.

H. R.

1

INTRODUCTION

> There are no abstract truths—no Mass-Man, no proletariat.
> There is only Man. When the Pulse has been nailed upon the
> crossbeams, lo, Reason gives up its viable breath and
> becomes a wandering ghostly Error. Truth and folly are ever
> about to expire, so that we, like our beloved Sancho Panza
> kneeling at the death-bed of Don Quixote, must always be
> ready to go out to receive the holy communion of cudgels and
> distaffs, for the rebirth of the Pulse, living anew, in our veins
> and bones, as the quickened Truth.
>
> Edward Dahlberg, *Do These Bones Live?* (New York, 1941).

Ever since democracy became a clear political conception in the
city-state of Athens, democratic philosophers have been faced
with the anomaly of the artist. It has seemed to them that the
artist, by his very nature, cannot be accommodated within the
structure of an egalitarian community. He is inevitably a social
misfit, to normal people a psychotic, and for rational thinkers
like Plato the only solution was to banish him from the community. A modern rationalist would probably recommend that
he should be cured of his psychosis.

There are two main problems: (1) What is it that seems to *separate* the artist from the rest of the community, making him unique among men? (2) What is it that nevertheless *reconciles* the community to this separatist individual—that is to say, what values does the artist contribute to the community that make the community accept or tolerate his presence among them?

The essays which are collected in this volume return again and again to these problems, and by way of introduction I should like to attempt a general summary of the view I have put forward.

We ought first to decide whether the artist is physically unique. We know that mankind is divisible into various distinct psychological types, and that these types have a basis in physiological factors. Is the artist such a type? There is a certain amount of evidence which suggests that he is. We know that some musicians possess what is called 'absolute pitch'. It is a natural disposition which is inherited and which cannot be acquired. A similar faculty in poets and plastic artists is not so commonly recognized, but nevertheless it exists. In poetry it is an absolute awareness of the identity of word and image, and in the plastic arts it probably takes the form of what we call 'an intuitive sense of proportion', with or without an intuitive sense of colour harmony, and these 'senses' are strictly analogous to the musician's absolute pitch. These facts, although incompletely investigated, must, I think, be admitted. But it must also be admitted that they are not essential. Several famous composers have been without absolute pitch, and there have certainly been poets without absolute identity of word and image—in fact, to insist on such an identity, in view of the limitations of language, would considerably restrict the range of poetry. One can also easily think of great painters whose colour sense has been defective, and of great architects who have had to rely on consciously applied canons of proportion. In the end, the most that one would be able to claim is that the possession of such unique gifts merely gives special quality to the work of a particular artist.

Apart from the occasional possession of such physiological peculiarities, it is obvious that the artist is not a separate psychological type. There are introvert and extravert artists, schizophrenic and manic-depressive artists. In fact, every psychological type is potentially an artist—which is only another way of agreeing with Eric Gill that every man is a special kind of artist.

The acceptance of this fact—and I for one do accept it—involves us logically in an admission that art is skill: a man does something so well that he is entitled to be called an artist. We are still left with a wide scope for argument, for we must ask what that something is: what is the purpose of that skill?

It was at this point that Gill and I, in our prolonged discussions, used to diverge, for I would insist that art is not merely skill to make, but also skill to express. Express what? Gill would ask, and if I was careless enough to use a phrase such as: 'To express his personality', Gill would be at me with the mallet and chisel he kept in his mind no less than in his hands, demanding if I had ever seen a personality, and how in God's name it could be expressed except in the making of something useful. And so the argument went on, to its inconclusive end. But I still maintain that there is a sense in which art is expression as well as making, and it is important that I should maintain my point, because it bears directly on this problem of the artist and society. For it is not sufficient to say that the artist is a skilled worker, and that he will always be valued by the community because his skill is useful. The truth is that the artist is very often (oftenest when he is greatest) offering something to the community which the community does not want to accept, which the community at first finds very unpalatable.

The mistaken presentation of my point of view, of which I have myself been guilty in the past, is to describe art as self-expression. If every artist merely expresses the uniqueness and separateness of his self, then art might be disruptive and anti-social. A lot of art in the past has been of that kind, and has given rise to the whole problem of 'dilettantism'. A social art can never be dilettante—dilettante art can never be social.

Obviously the great artist who is not merely making something, like a carpenter or a cobbler, but expressing something, like Shakespeare or Michelangelo or Beethoven, is expressing something bigger than his self. Self-expression, like self-seeking, is an illusion. It is the action of an individual who pits himself against the community, who says I am bigger, or better, or stronger than other men, and will therefore enslave them, make them serve my individual purposes. But a democracy would be right to resent the presence of such individuals in its midst, for democracy starts from the proposition that all men are equal—if this dogma is not accepted, then the word democracy is being used in a sense which I do not regard as legitimate. The word democracy should always imply, not only liberty and fraternity, but also equality.

Society expects something more than self-expression from its artists, and in the case of great artists such as those I have mentioned, it gets something more. It gets something which might be called life-expression. But the 'life' to be expressed, the life which is expressed in great art, is precisely the life of the community, the organic group consciousness. It is the artist's business to make the group aware of its unity, its community. He can do this because he, more than other men, has access to the common unconsciousness, to the collective instincts which underlie the brittle surface of convention and normality. I cannot say why the artist should have this gift, any more than I can say why he has absolute pitch, etc. It is probably a consequence of his early upbringing, the actual course of his adaptation to society in earliest infancy—the complicated process which psychoanalysis is slowly reconstructing. Whatever the explanation, the function of the artist in modern society is much the same as that of the medicine-man or magician in a primitive society: he is the man who mediates between our individual consciousness and the collective unconsciousness, and thus ensures social re-integration. It is only in the degree that this mediation is successful that a true democracy is possible.

This office of mediation cannot be forced upon the artist. His function is catalytic—he aids the social revolution without himself undergoing any change, without being absorbed by the social substance. That, it seems to me, is the central doctrine of Wordsworth's *Preface to the Lyrical Ballads*, which is probably the most careful definition of the poet's function ever made. I do not think there are any essential problems of the artist in a modern society which we do not find anticipated there. The *Preface* was first published in 1800—at a time, that is to say, very comparable to our own. Two years earlier, in 1798, Wordsworth's political consciousness had reached a crisis—he had experienced a final disillusionment with the French Revolution. The crisis for so many poets and artists of today is of exactly the same nature. The signing of the pact between Germany and Russia was probably the breaking-point, but the Moscow trials and executions, and a gradual realization that the Russian Revolution had followed precisely the same course as the French Revolution, had created a psychological tension which was bound to break sooner or later. Hundreds of poets and artists of every kind found that their idealism was suddenly dead—betrayed by the cynical politicians who had for so long deceived them. Poets who now turn in on themselves, to discover the truth about the poet and society, begin to tread the same labyrinth as Wordsworth. They might save themselves much trouble by re-reading the *Preface*, weighing it phrase by phrase.

Two particularly relevant phrases to which I should like to draw attention are based on the words 'pleasure' and 'tranquillity'. The second phrase is the more familiar, though it is nearly always distorted in quotation: '*poetry takes its origin from emotion recollected in tranquillity*'. The first phrase has not caught the popular imagination so readily, though it is no less striking: '*We have no sympathy but what is propagated by pleasure.*'

This second phrase, explains Wordsworth, refers to 'the grand elementary principle of pleasure, by which (man) knows, and feels, and lives, and moves . . . we have no knowledge, that is, no general principle drawn from the contemplation of particular facts, but what has been built up by pleasure, and exists in us by pleasure alone'. Further, 'wherever we sympathize with pain, it will be found that the sympathy is produced and carried on by subtle combinations with pleasure'.

This statement, which might have been derived from Epicurus or Lucretius, is also remarkable as an anticipation of Freud's pleasure-principle. (Cf.: 'We may put the question whether a main purpose is discernible in the operation of the mental apparatus; and our first approach to an answer is that this purpose is directed to the attainment of pleasure. It seems that our entire psychic activity is bent upon *procuring pleasure* and *avoiding pain*, that it is automatically regulated by the pleasure-principle.'[1]) But we are concerned now with the function which Wordsworth gives to this pleasure-principle in the process of poetic activity.[2]

It is a function that enables us to return to the artist the uniqueness which we began by taking away from him. Gill went so far as to suggest that there is no essential difference between

---

[1] *Introductory Lectures on Psychoanalysis*, London, 1933, p. 298.

[2] According to Wordsworth, the following stages are involved:

(1) The origin of the process: emotion recollected in tranquillity.

(2) Contemplation of this recollection continued until, 'by a species of reaction', the tranquillity gradually disappears and is replaced by

(3) an emotion, *kindred* to that which was before the subject of contemplation.

(4) Composition may then occur inducing

(5) a state of enjoyment whatever the nature of the emotion that is being experienced by the poet.

the artist and the artisan—between, shall we say, Shakespeare and the carpenter who made his second-best bed. And he came to the conclusion that there may not have been much difference in the quality of their skill: the carpentry of the plays is not above criticism, and the second-best bed was well enough made to be specified in the poet's last will and testament. What, then, did Shakespeare possess that was denied to this carpenter?

There is no mystery about it: it was the capacity to work in psychological material, to make a work of art out of more than words: out of human desires and emotion, fears and fantasies. And that is where the peculiarity and what we recognize as the 'greatness' of the artist comes in: for these materials cannot be worked superficially, on the surface. The artist must be ready to delve below the level of normal consciousness, the crust of conventional thought and behaviour, into his own unconscious, and into the collective unconscious of his group or race. It is a painful experience: creative work on this level is only done at a cost of mental anguish. This is where Wordsworth's perception of the realities of poetic composition becomes so acute; for there is no doubt that the poet's creation, his sympathetic penetration into the tragic significance of life, however painful, 'is produced and carried on by subtle combinations with pleasure'. The artist is always something of a masochist.

He is also an escapist. Wordsworth does not define what he means by tranquillity, but his meaning is obvious enough if we remember his social behaviour and his practice in composition, as described by his sister Dorothy and other witnesses. Tranquillity, for Wordsworth, meant literally a flight from society; and the actual moment of composition meant a flight from even those members of his household with whom he habitually dwelt.

Wordsworth's precept has been powerfully reinforced nearer our time by Rilke, in those *Letters to a Young Poet* which are so full of profound wisdom. 'I can give you no other advice,' said Rilke to his correspondent, 'than this: retire into yourself and probe the depths from which your life springs up. . . . For the creative artist must be a world unto himself and find everything in himself and in Nature, of which he is part and parcel.' And again: 'Love your loneliness, and *endure the pain* which it causes you *with harmonious lamentations (schoenklingender Klage).*' The word *Einsamkeit* (loneliness, solitariness, tranquillity) recurs like a refrain through all these letters, and indeed through all Rilke's work. It will be remembered that Milton also spoke movingly of 'a calm and pleasing solitariness'.

Rilke, it might be objected, was writing in 1903, when solitariness could be found, if not easily, at least possibly. But that artificial isolation, which I have called fortress-solitude, is not the same thing as Rilke's *Einsamkeit* or Wordsworth's tranquillity or Milton's solitariness. It is not, in Rilke's phrase, bound to Nature—by which he means a natural way of living. In such fast seclusion the poet cannot be, in Wordsworth's phrase, 'a man speaking to men'. It may seem unreasonable to non-poetic people, but what the poet nevertheless demands is a kind of society in which tranquillity, withdrawal, is a natural right. He must be able to go into the press and out of it as easily as he passes from his own house into the street. The charge he makes against the modern world is that it has invaded his house of quiet, invaded it with cares and rumours, insistent politics and totalitarian wars.

The poet is therefore compelled to demand, *for poetic reasons*, that the world shall be changed. It cannot be said that his demand is unreasonable: it is the first condition of his existence as a poet.

The changes promised by the existing political parties have no appeal to the poet. They do not guarantee his solitude. They all imply a more exacting social contract, a more complete surrender of individual liberty: surrender to the state, surrender to the curiosity of the Press, surrender to mass opinions and mass standards. If poetry is ever again to be more than 'self-expression' the direction must be reversed—political power must be distributed and broken down into human, tangible units. Economic responsibility must be accepted by the worker. Financial power divorced from production must be altogether excluded from society. Productive labour must be recognized as the basic reality, and honoured as such. That is why the poet must be an anarchist. He has no other choice. He may temporize with liberalism, with democratic socialism, with state socialism; and in peaceful times any of these political systems may be persuaded to patronize culture, including poetry. But they cannot guarantee the creative activity of the poet. They cannot admit the solitude of any of their citizens, for solitude is a withdrawal from the social contract, a denial of the principle of collectivism. It is a bitter lesson to learn, for those poets who have put their faith in the non-poetic prophets—in Marx, in Lenin, in Stalin. Poets should not go outside their own ranks for a policy; for poetry is its own politics.

Shelley called poets the unacknowledged legislators of the world, and the epithet was well chosen. The catalyst is unchanged, unabsorbed; its activity therefore not acknowledged. It is peculiarly difficult for the artist in society to accept this thankless task: to stand apart, and yet to mediate: to communicate to society something as essential as bread or water, and yet to be able to do so only from a position of insulation, of disaffection. Society will never understand or love the artist, because it will never appreciate his indifference, his so-called objectivity. But the artist must learn to love and understand the society that renounces him. He must accept the contrary experience, and drink, with Socrates, the deadly cup.

2

TO HELL WITH CULTURE

When will revolutionary leaders realize that 'culture' is dope, a worse dope than religion; for even if it were true that religion is the opiate of the people, it is worse to poison yourself than to be poisoned, and suicide is more dishonourable than murder. To hell with culture, culture as a thing added like a sauce to otherwise unpalatable stale fish!

Eric Gill

The cultured Greeks, it seems, had no word for culture. They had good architects, good sculptors, good poets, just as they had good craftsmen and good statesmen. They knew that their way of life was a good way of life, and they were willing if necessary to fight to defend it. But it would never have occurred to them that they had a separate commodity, culture—something to be given a trade-mark by their academicians, something to be acquired by superior people with sufficient time and money, something to be exported to foreign countries along with figs and olives. It wasn't even an invisible export: it was something natural if it existed at all—something of which they were unconscious, something as instinctive as their language or the complexion of their skins. It could not even be described as a by-product of their way of life: it was that way of life itself.

It was the Romans, the first large-scale capitalists in Europe, who turned culture into a commodity. They began by importing culture—Greek culture—and then they grew autarkic and produced their own brand. As they extended their empire, they dumped their culture on the conquered nations. Roman architecture, Roman literature, Roman manners—these set a standard to which all newly civilized people aspired. When a Roman poet like Ovid talks about a cultured man, there is already the sense of something polished, refined, a veneer on the surface of an otherwise rough humanity. It would not have occurred to a refined Roman of this sort that the craftsmen of his time had any contribution to make to the finer values of life. Nor had they—Roman pottery, for example, may be cultured, but it is dull and degraded.

Culture, we are told, went underground in the Dark Ages, and it was a long time before it came to the surface again. The next epoch, known as the Middle Ages, is rivalled only by the Greek Age; but, oddly enough, it too was not conscious of its culture. Its architects were foremen builders, its sculptors were masons, its illuminators and painters were clerks. They had no word for art in the sense of our 'fine arts': art was all that was pleasing to the sight: a cathedral, a candlestick, a chessman, a cheese-press.

But the Middle Ages came to an end, and with them the guild system and the making of things for use. Certain clever people began to grab things—church property, common land, minerals, especially gold. They began to make things in order to acquire more than they could use, a surplus which they could convert into gold; and because they couldn't eat gold, or build houses with it, they lent it to other people who were in need of it and charged them rent or interest. And thus the capitalist system came into existence, and with it the thing we call 'culture'.

The first recorded use of the word in its modern sense is 1510, just when capitalism began to get going. It is the time of the Revival of Learning and the Renaissance, and those two movements signify the very essence of culture for all educated people, even unto the present day. But it was not until the beginning of the nineteenth century, the period of the Industrial Revolution, that culture became finally divorced from work. So long as people made things by hand, certain traditional ways of making them persisted, and were good. It was only when things began to be made by machines that the traditions inherent, as it were, in the minds and muscles of the handworker, finally disappeared.

To take the place of this instinctive tradition, the industrialists introduced certain new standards. They might be merely standards of utility and cheapness—that is to say, of profitableness; but since sensitive people were not satisfied with these, the manufacturers began to look back into the past, to collect and imitate the good things which had been made by their ancestors. If you knew all about the things of the past, you were recognized as a man of taste, and the sum of the nation's 'tastes' was its 'culture'. Matthew Arnold, in fact, defined culture as 'the acquainting ourselves with the best that has been known and said in the world'. And with Matthew Arnold, the Prince Consort and the Great Exhibition, we reach the peak point of the English cult of culture. After the 'sixties its self-consciousness became too obvious, and we entered a period of decadence—Pre-Raphaelitism, the Yellow Book, Oscar Wilde, and Aubrey Beardsley—until the First World War came and gave a final push to the whole rotten fabric.

For the last quarter of a century we have been trying to pick up the pieces: we have had lectures and exhibitions, museums and art galleries, adult education and cheap books, and even an

International Committee for Intellectual Co-operation sponsored by the League of Nations. But it was all a beating on a hollow drum, and it required a Second World War to bring us up finally against the realities of this question as of so many others.

A democratic culture—*that is not the same thing as a democracy plus culture.* The first important point that I must make, and keep on stressing, is that culture in a natural society will not be a separate and distinguishable thing—a body of learning that can be put into books and museums and mugged up in your spare time. Just because it will not exist as a separate entity, it would be better to stop using the word 'culture'. We shall not need it in the future and it will only confuse the present issue. Culture belongs to the past: the future will not be conscious of its culture.

The values which I am concerned with in this essay—values which we call 'the beautiful'—were not invented in ancient Athens or anywhere else. They are part of the structure of the universe and of our consciousness of that structure. To argue this point fully would carry us too far into the obscure regions of philosophy, and I have written enough about it in my more technical books. But what I mean, in simple language, is that we should not be pleased with the way certain things look unless our physical organs and the senses which control them were so constituted as to be pleased with certain definite proportions, relations, rhythms, harmonies, and so on. When we say, for example, that two colours 'clash', we are not expressing a personal opinion: there is a definite scientific reason for the disagreeable impression they create, and it could no doubt be expressed in a mathematical formula. Again, when a printer decides to impose the type on a page so as to leave margins of a definite proportion, he is trusting to his eye, which tells him by its muscular tensions that this particular arrangement is easeful. These are very elementary examples, and when large paintings or poems or musical compositions are in question, the whole business is infinitely more complicated. But, in general, we see that certain proportions in nature (in crystals, plants, the human figure, etc.) are 'right', and we carry over these proportions into the things we make—not deliberately, but instinctively.

For our present purposes that is all we need to know of the science of aesthetics. There is an order in Nature and the order of Society should be a reflection of it, not only in our way of living, but also in our way of doing and making. If we follow this natural order in all the ways of our life, we shall not need to talk about culture. We shall have it without being conscious of it.

But how are we to attain the natural order of making things, which is my particular concern in this essay?

Obviously, we can't make things naturally in unnatural surroundings. We can't do things properly unless we are properly fed and properly housed. We must also be properly equipped with the necessary tools, and then left alone to get on with the job.

In other words, before we can make things naturally, we must establish the natural order in society, which for my present purposes I assume is what we all mean by a democracy. But it is useless to talk about a democratic art or a democratic literature until we are in fact a democracy.

Seventy years ago Walt Whitman wrote in his *Democratic Vistas*:

> 'We have frequently printed the word Democracy. Yet I cannot too often repeat that it is a word the real gist of which still sleeps, quite unawakened, notwithstanding the resonance and the many angry tempests out of which its syllables have come, from pen and tongue. It is a great word, whose history, I suppose, remains unwritten, because that history has yet to be enacted.'

Democracy is still a great word, and in spite of many wordy

prophets who have used it since Whitman's time, its gist still sleeps, its history is still unenacted. Nothing is more absurd, among all the political absurdities committed by fascists and Nazis, than their assumption that democracy is a system that has been tried and has failed. Democracy has been promulgated and its principles endlessly proclaimed; but in no country in the world has it ever, for more than a brief space of a few months, been put into practice. For democracy requires three conditions for its fulfilment, and until all three conditions are satisfied, it cannot be said to exist. It is only necessary to state these conditions to show that democracy never has existed in modern times:

The first condition of democracy is that *all production should be for use, and not for profit.*

The second condition is that *each should give according to his ability, and each receive according to his needs.*

The third condition is that *the workers in each industry should collectively own and control that industry.*

It is not my business in this particular essay to defend the conception of democracy underlying these conditions. Nevertheless I would claim that it is the classical conception of democracy as gradually evolved by its philosophers—by Rousseau, Jefferson, Lincoln, Proudhon, Owen, Ruskin, Marx, Morris, Kropotkin, and whoever else was democratic in his heart no less than in his head. What I intend to demonstrate here is that the higher values of life, the democratic equivalent of the civilization of Greece or of the Middle Ages, cannot be achieved unless by democracy we mean a form of society in which all these three conditions are satisfied.

I think it will be generally admitted that production for use and not for profit is the basic economic doctrine of socialism. The opponents of socialism might argue that only a lunatic would neglect to take into consideration the needs of the public. But that is to miss the whole point of the statement. Capitalists do, of course, produce for use, and even invent uses for which to produce—in their own language, they create a demand. By their intensive methods of production and their extensive methods of publicity they have keyed up the machinery of production to unimagined levels, and up to a point mankind has benefited from the resulting plethora. Unfortunately capitalism has not been able to solve the problem of supplying the consumer with sufficient purchasing power to absorb this plethora: it could only invent various methods of restricting production so as to prevent a plethora.

Capitalism can produce the goods, even if it cannot sell them. But what kind of goods? It is here that we have to introduce our aesthetic criterion. Let us first note that the quality of the goods so lavishly produced under capitalism varies enormously. Whatever you take—carpets or chairs, houses or clothes, cigarettes or sausages, you will find that there are not one but twenty or thirty grades—something very good and efficient at the top of the scale, and something very cheap and nasty at the bottom of the scale. And pyramid-like, the bottom of the scale is enormously bigger than the top.

Take the case of the chair you are sitting on as you read this book. It may be one of three things: (1) a decent well-made chair, inherited from your great-great-grandmother; (2) a decent well-made chair which you bought at an expensive shop; or (3) an indifferent, uncomfortable chair, shabby after a year's use, which was the best you could afford. (There are some subsidiary categories—expensive chairs that are also uncomfortable, for example; and moderately comfortable seats in public vehicles.)

Production for profit means that, at whatever cost to the comfort, appearance and durability of the chair, the capitalist must put chairs on the market to suit every kind of purse. And since the chair will be competing with other needs—carpets, clocks and sewing-machines—it must cost as little as possible even on the low scale of purchasing power at which he is aiming. Hence the capitalist must progressively lower the quality of the materials he is using: he must use cheap wood and little of it, cheap springs and cheap upholstery. He must evolve a design that is cheap to produce and easy to sell, which means that he must disguise his cheap materials with veneer and varnish and other shams. Even if he is aiming at the top market, he still has to remember his margin of profits; and as the size of the market shrinks, and mass production becomes less possible, this margin has to be increased. That is to say, the difference between the intrinsic value of the materials used and the price charged to the consumer has to be bigger; and the subterfuges necessary to disguise this difference have to be cleverer.

It is then the capitalist has to put on, among other things, a bit of culture—a claw-and-ball foot in the manner of Chippendale, a wriggly bit of scrollwork in papier-mâché, an inlay of mother-of-pearl. In extreme cases he must 'distress' the piece—that is to say, employ a man to throw bolts and nails at the chair until it has been knocked about enough to look 'antique'.

Such is production for profit. By production for use we mean a system which will have only two considerations in mind— function and fulfilment. You want a chair to relax in—very well, we shall discover what are the best angles to allow a man's limbs to rest freely and without strain. We shall next consider which would be the most suitable materials to use in the manufacture of such a chair, bearing in mind, not only the purpose the chair has to serve, but also the other furniture with which the chair will be associated. Then, and then only, we shall design a chair to meet all these requirements. Finally we shall set about making the chair, and when it is made to our satisfaction, we shall offer it to you in exchange for the tokens which represent the good work which, all the time we were making the chair, you were doing for the community at your particular job.

That is the economic process under socialism. But I am

supposed to be writing about spiritual values—about beauty and all that sort of thing, and where do they come in? We have produced a chair which is strong and comfortable, but is it a work of art?

The answer, according to my philosophy of art, is Yes. If an object is made of appropriate materials to an appropriate design and perfectly fulfils its function, then we need not worry any more about its aesthetic value: it is *automatically* a work of art. Fitness for function is the modern definition of the eternal quality we call beauty, and this fitness for function is the inevitable result of an economy directed to use and not to profit.

Incidentally, we may note that when the profit system has to place function before profit, as in the production of an aeroplane or a racing-car, it also inevitably produces a work of art. But the question to ask is: why are not all the things produced under capitalism as beautiful as its aeroplanes and racing-cars?

The second condition of democracy is expressed in the Marxian slogan: 'From each according to his ability, to each according to his needs.'

This condition is linked to the one we have already discussed. To take the question of ability first. A profit system of production subordinates the person to the job. In a rough-and-ready way it sorts people out according to their ability: that is to say, it continues to employ a man only so long as he is capable of doing the job efficiently, and only so long as there is a job to do. It rarely asks whether a particular man would be better at another job, and it gives that man little or no opportunity of finding out whether he could do another job better. Capitalism is concerned with labour only as a power element, the partner of steam and electricity. And since the cost of this power has to be reckoned against the possible profits, capitalism does all it can to reduce that cost.

One way of reducing the cost is to increase the quantity of

work per human unit. Capitalism (and state socialism as established in Russia) introduces the time element into the calculation of results. The best riveter is the man who can fix the greatest number of rivets in a given time. The best miner is the man who can dig out the greatest quantity of coal in a given time. This time criterion is extended to all forms of production, and it is always at war with the criterion of quality. When the work is purely mechanical, the qualitative element may not be compromised. A quick riveter may also be a good riveter. But if the work requires any considerable degree of skill, care or deliberation, then the quality will decline in inverse ratio to the speed of production. This applies, not only to 'artistic' work such as painting and sculpture, but also to 'practical' work such as grinding the cylinders of an aero-engine or ploughing a field.

From each according to his ability can be replaced by another familiar phrase—equality of opportunity. In a natural society it should be possible for people to sort themselves out so that every man and woman is doing the job for which he or she feels naturally qualified; and if, in this respect, nature needs a little assistance, it can be provided by schools and technical colleges which will enable young people to discover themselves and their abilities.

That half of the slogan does not present much difficulty: it is obviously reasonable that the right man should have the right job, and that he should do that job to the best of his ability. But then we say: 'to each according to his needs', and this is the more important half, and the essentially democratic half, of the socialist doctrine.

Let us ask: what are the needs of each one of us? Sufficient food and clothing, adequate housing—a certain minimum of these necessities should be the inalienable right of every member of the community. Until it can provide these minimum necessities, a society must be branded as inhuman and inefficient.

And that is perhaps all that early socialists like Marx and Engels meant by the phrase 'to each according to his needs'. But the underlying assumption of this essay is that in any civilization worth living in, the needs of man are not merely material. He hungers for other things—for beauty, for companionship, for joy. These, too, a natural society must provide.

We have already seen that by establishing a system of production for use we shall inevitably secure the first of these spiritual needs—beauty. To see how the other spiritual values will be secured we must turn to the third condition of democracy—workers' ownership of industry.

This is a controversial issue, even within the democratic ranks. Since that fatal day in 1872 when Marx scuttled the First International, the socialist movement has been split into two irreconcilable camps. The fundamental nature of the division has been hidden by a confusion of names and a multiplicity of leagues, alliances, federations and societies. But the issue is simply whether industry is to be controlled from the bottom upwards, by the workers and their elected delegates; or whether it is to be centralized and controlled from the top, by an abstraction we call the state, but which in effect means a small and exclusive class of bureaucrats.

The historical fact that everywhere in the north of Europe—Germany, Scandinavia, France and Great Britain—the authoritarian or bureaucratic conception of socialism triumphed should not blind us to the still living issue. For this 'conceptual' triumph somehow has not brought with it what we mean by a democracy. Indeed, in most of the countries named it brought about just the opposite phenomenon—the anti-democratic state of Hitler, Mussolini, Stalin and Franco.

Do not let us deceive ourselves in thinking that fascism anywhere in the world is merely a temporary phase of reactionaryism. Reactionary it is, in the deepest sense of the word, for it denies the advance of the human spirit; and it offers sinister accommodations to the industrial capitalists who have been democracy's most bitter enemies. But in many of its features it is but a development or adaptation of that authoritarian form of socialism which Marx made the predominant form of socialism. It even claimed the name of socialism in Germany, and it was somewhat unfortunate that this fact was disguised in the popular contraction: Nazi. Hitler's New Order was socialist in that it established a centralized state control of all production. It was socialist in that it established a system of social security— guaranteed employment, fair rates of wages, organized amenities of various kinds. It was socialist in that it subordinated the financial system to the industrial system. In many ways it was professedly socialist, but it remained profoundly undemocratic. Because whatever it gave in the shape of social security, it took away in spiritual liberty.

The Nazis were very culture-conscious—as culture-conscious as Matthew Arnold and all our Victorian forefathers. But the more conscious they became of culture, the less capable they were of producing it. Nazi Germany, in the ten years of its supremacy and intensive cultivation of the arts, was not able to produce for the admiration of the world a single artist of any kind. Most of its great writers and painters—Thomas Mann, Franz Werfel, Oskar Kokoschka and many others were driven into exile. A few great artists who remained in Germany—the composer Strauss, for example—were too old to produce any new work of significance, and too indifferent to the political order to want to produce anything at all. A few writers of integrity and genius remained in Germany—I am thinking particularly of Hans Carossa and Ernst Robert Curtius—but they lived in spiritual agony. For this general impotence the Nazi leaders may have offered the excuse of war and revolution, but other wars and revolutions have been an immediate inspiration to poets and painters. The great Romantic Movement in literature, for example, was directly inspired by the French Revolution, and all the storm and stress of the wars that followed could not diminish its force.

The position in Italy was exactly the same, and showed in addition that the time factor makes no difference. The Fascists were in power for twenty years, but in all that time not a single work of art of universal significance came from their country— nothing but bombast and vulgarity.

There is only one explanation of this failure of the Fascist and Nazi Revolutions to inspire a great art, and I cannot describe it better than in the words of Giovanni Gentile, a liberal philosopher who sold himself to the fascist régime. Speaking to an audience of teachers in Trieste shortly after that city had fallen into Italian hands at the end of the First World War he declared: 'Spiritual activity works only in the plenitude of freedom.' It was a fine moment for the Italian people, and this was a fine sentiment to match the occasion. More than twenty years passed, and Gentile served Mussolini as his Minister of Education for most of that time, and did as much as anyone to give fascism a decent covering of intellectual respectability. As he surveyed the tyranny he had helped to establish and saw all around him a spiritual poverty in keeping with an economic poverty, it is possible that this sad and disillusioned man repeated, in a whisper which was only heard in the secret recesses of his own mind: Spiritual activity works only in the plenitude of freedom.

One thing must be admitted: the lack of any spiritual activity in Germany and Italy was not due to a lack of official encouragement. In Germany there was a complex organization, the Reichskulturkammer, charged with the specific task of supervising cultural activities of every kind, and in Italy there was a similar display of state patronage. Outside the fascist countries there was a parallel activity in Russia, and in the U.S.A. there was the Federal Arts Project. This latter organization had a different aim: to relieve distress among artists rather than to encourage the production of a national type of art. But all four types of state patronage illustrated the same truth—that no amount of sauce will disguise the staleness of the underlying fish. You cannot buy the spiritual values which make the greatness of a nation's art: you cannot even cultivate them unless you prepare the soil. And that soil is freedom—not Freedom with a capital F, not an abstraction of any kind, but simply 'letting alone'.

'Letting alone' is not the same as 'laissez faire'. A person is not left alone if he has a cupboard full of cares. He must be left alone with sufficient food and shelter to safeguard his health, and he must be left alone with sufficient material to work with. Another French phrase, lacher prise, better expresses this idea.

To keep a class of people in comfort and then let them do what they please offends the sense of social equity—every dustman might then set up as an artist. But that is not exactly what I propose. I have said: To hell with culture; and to this consignment we might add another: To hell with the artist. Art as a separate profession is merely a consequence of culture as a separate entity. In a natural society there will be no precious or privileged beings called artists: there will only be workers. Or, if you prefer Gill's more paradoxical statement of the same truth: in a natural society there will be no despised and unprivileged beings called workers: there will only be artists. 'The artist is not a special kind of man, but every man is a special kind of artist.'[1]

But among workers there are various degrees of ability. And the people capable of recognizing this ability are the workers themselves in their several professions. For example, architects and engineers will know which few individuals among them design so superlatively well that they deserve, for the common

---

[1] Gill took this paradox from the writings of another wise man, Dr. Ananda Coomaraswamy, and Coomaraswamy in his turn seems to have taken it from Sri Aurobindo; it sums up in one sentence the teachings of William Morris and the practice of the medieval guild system.

good, to be exempted from routine tasks and encouraged to devote their energies to those types of work that are not so much utilitarian as 'creative'—that is to say, expressive of their own inventive intuitions or perhaps of collective needs—needs which are inarticulate until the artist gives them actuality.

It is the same with every other type of artist—the painter and the sculptor no less than the architect and the engineer. The possible exception is the poet, the 'divine literatus' to whom Whitman gave such a vital function in the democratic vista. There is no basic profession which stands in the same relation to poetry as building does to architecture. Writing is, of course, a profession, and in a democratic society it should have its appropriate guild or collective—as it has in Russia today. Once it is free from the rivalries and log-rolling which accompany writing for profit (or writing on the backs of advertisements, as Chesterton called journalism), a Writers' Guild might be entrusted with the economic organization of this particular kind of work; but genius will often elude its systematic survey. Against this eventuality there can be no social safeguard. There are certain types of genius which are always in advance of the general level of sensibility—even the general level of professional sensibility. In the past such men have been frustrated or have been starved. In a natural society they will at least avoid the second fate.

Production for use, mutual aid, workers' control—these are the slogans of democracy, and these are the slogans of a creative civilization. There is nothing mysterious or difficult about such a civilization; indeed, some of the primitive civilizations still existing in remote corners of the world, and many primitive civilizations of the past, including that of prehistoric man, deserve to be called creative. What they make, if it is only a plaited basket or an unpainted pot, they make with instinctive rightness and directness. It is impossible to compare such primitive communities with our own highly organized modes of living, but their social economy in its simple way answers to our slogans. Production is for use and not for profit; and all work is done without compulsion for the general benefit of the community. On their simple level of living there is ample social security, and no man sells his labour to a middleman or boss: work is either individual or communal, and in either case it is free from the dispiriting influences of slavery and manumission.

But our societies are not primitive and there is no need to become primitive in order to secure the essentials of democratic liberty. We want to retain all our scientific and industrial triumphs—electric power, machine tools, mass production and the rest. We do not propose to revert to the economy of the handloom and the plough—ideal as this may seem in retrospect. We propose that the workers and technicians who have made the modern instruments of production should control them—control their use and determine the flow of their production. It can be done. Russia has shown that the essential organization can be created, and we should not be blinded to the significance of that great achievement by the perversion it has suffered at the hands of bureaucrats. For a brief spell democratic Spain showed us that workers' control could be an efficient reality. Workers' control can be established in every country, and there is not much point in discussing the finer values of civilization until that essential change has been effected.

The fundamental truth about economics is that the methods and instruments of production, freely used and fairly used, are capable of giving every human being a decent standard of living. The factors which obstruct the free and fair use of the methods and instruments of production are the factors which must disappear before a natural society can be established, Whatever these factors are—an obsolete financial system, the private ownership of property, rent and usury—they are anti-democratic factors, and prevent the establishment of a natural society and consequently prevent the establishment of a creative civilization.

Economics are outside the scope of this essay, but I cannot avoid them. Unless the present economic system is abolished, its roots eradicated and all its intricate branches lopped, the first conditions for a democratic alternative to the fake culture of our present civilization are not satisfied. For this reason one cannot be very specific about the features of a democratic culture. Engineers and designers can make the working drawings for a motor-car, and granted the right kind of machinery, they can be sure that the type of car they have designed will run when it is completed. But they cannot predict where that car will travel. A democratic culture is the journey a democratic society will make when once it has been established. If it is well made we know that our democratic society will travel far. And with the man for whom it was made at the wheel, we can be sure that it will travel in the right directon, discovering new countries, new prospects, new climates. We have already taken brief glimpses down these democratic vistas; let us now take a backward glance at the dump we propose to leave behind us.

I write, not as a philistine, but as a man who could not only claim to be cultured in the accepted sense of the word, but who has actually devoted most of his life to cultural things—to the practice of the arts of the present and the elucidation of the arts of the past. My philosophy is a direct product of my aesthetic experience, and I believe that life without art would be a graceless and brutish existence. I could not live without the spiritual values of art. I know that some people are insensitive to these values, but before allowing myself to pity or despise such people, I try to imagine how they got themselves into such a poor state of mind. The more I consider such people, the more clearly I begin to perceive that though there may be a minority who have been hopelessly brutalized by their environment and upbringing, the great majority are not insensitive, but indifferent. They have sensibility, but the thing we call culture does not stir them. Architecture and sculpture, painting and poetry, are not the immediate concerns of their lives. They are therefore not sensibly moved by the baroque rhetoric of St. Paul's, or the painted ceiling of the Sistine Chapel, or any of the minor monuments of our culture. If they go into a museum or art gallery, they move about with dead eyes: they have strayed among people who do not speak their language, with whom they cannot by any means communicate.

Now the common assumption is that this strayed riveter, as we may call him, should set about it and learn the language of this strange country—that he should attend museum lectures and adult education classes in the little spare time he has, and so gradually lift himself on to the cultured level. Our whole educational system is built on that assumption, and very few democrats would be found to question it. And yet a moment's consideration should convince us that an educational system that is built on such an assumption is fundamentally wrong, and fundamentally undemocratic. Our riveter has probably strayed from a cheerless street in Birmingham, where he inhabits a mean little house furnished with such shoddy comforts as he has been able to afford out of his inadequate wage. I need not pursue the man's life in all its dreary detail: there he stands, typical of millions of workers in this country, his clumsy boots on the parquet floor, and you are asking him to appreciate a painting by Botticelli or a bust by Bernini, a Spanish textile or a fine piece of Limoges enamel. If drink is the shortest road out of Manchester, there is a possibility that art may be the shortest road out of Birmingham; but it will not be a crowded road, and only a very odd and eccentric worker will be found to respond to the aesthetic thrills that run down a cultured spine.

There are cultured people who, realizing this fact, are honest enough to abandon their democratic pretensions—they put up an impenetrable barrier between the people and art, between the worker and 'culture'. It is much better, they say, 'that civilization should be retained in the hands of those persons to whom it professionally belongs. Until they are educated, and unless they are, it will be one worker in a million who wants to read a modern poem.'[2]

Such people are right, and such people are wrong. They are right to assume that an impenetrable barrier exists between their culture and the worker: they are wrong to imagine that the worker has no cultural sensibility. The worker has as much latent sensibility as any human being, but that sensibility can only be awakened when meaning is restored to his daily work and he is allowed to create his own culture.

Do not let us be deceived by the argument that culture is the same for all time—that art is a unity and beauty an absolute value. If we are going to talk about abstract conceptions like beauty, then we can freely grant that they are absolute and eternal. But abstract conceptions are not works of art. Works of art are things of use—houses and their furniture, for example; and if, like sculpture and poetry, they are not things of immediate use, then they should be things consonant with the things we use—that is to say, part of our daily life, tuned to our daily habits, accessible to our daily needs. It is not until art expresses the immediate hopes and aspirations of humanity that it acquires its social relevance.

A culture begins with simple things—with the way the potter moulds the clay on his wheel, the way a weaver threads his yarns, the way the builder builds his house. Greek culture did not begin with the Parthenon: it began with a whitewashed hut on a hillside. Culture has always developed as an infinitely slow but sure refinement and elaboration of simple things— refinement and elaboration of speech, refinement and elaboration of shapes, refinement and elaboration of proportions, with

<hr>

[2] Sacheverell Sitwell, *Sacred and Profane Love*, p. 88.

the original purity persisting right through. A democratic culture will begin in a similar way. We shall not revert to the peasant's hut or the potter's wheel. We shall begin with the elements of modern industry—electric power, metal alloys, cement, the tractor and the aeroplane. We shall consider these things as the raw materials of a civilization and we shall work out their appropriate use and appropriate forms, without reference to the lath and plaster of the past.

Today we are bound hand and foot to the past. Because property is a sacred thing and land values a source of untold wealth, our houses must be crowded together and our streets must follow their ancient illogical meanderings. Because houses must be built at the lowest possible cost to allow the highest possible profit, they are denied the art and science of the architect. Because everything we buy for use must be sold for profit, and because there must always be this profitable margin between cost and price, our pots and our pans, our furniture and our clothes, have the same shoddy consistency, the same competitive cheapness. The whole of our capitalist culture is one immense veneer: a surface refinement hiding the cheapness and shoddiness at the heart of things.

To hell with such a culture! To the rubbish-heap and furnace with it all! Let us celebrate the democratic revolution creatively. Let us build cities that are not too big, but spacious, with traffic flowing freely through their leafy avenues, with children playing safely in their green and flowery parks, with people living happily in bright efficient houses. Let us place our factories and workshops where natural conditions of supply make their location most convenient—the necessary electric power can be laid on anywhere. Let us balance agriculture and industry, town and country—let us do all these sensible and elementary things and then let us talk about our culture.

A culture of pots and pans! some of my readers may cry contemptuously. I do not despise a culture of pots and pans, because, as I have already said, the best civilizations of the past may be judged by their pots and pans. But what I am now asserting, as a law of history no less than as a principle of social economy, is that until a society can produce beautiful pots and pans as naturally as it grows potatoes, it will be incapable of those higher forms of art which in the past have taken the form of temples and cathedrals, epics and dramas.

As for the past, let the past take care of itself. I know that there is such a thing as tradition, but in so far as it is valuable it is a body of technical knowledge—the mysteries of the old guilds— and can safely be entrusted to the care of the new guilds. There is a traditional way of thatching haystacks and a traditional way of writing sonnets: they can be learned by any apprentice. If I am told that this is not the profoundest meaning of the word trad- ition, I will not be obtuse; but I will merely suggest that the state of the world today is a sufficient comment on those traditional embodiments of wisdom, ecclesiastical or academic, which we are expected to honour. The cultural problem, we are told by these traditionalists, is at bottom a spiritual, even a religious one. But this is not true. At least, it is no truer of the cultural problem than of the economic problem, or any of the other problems that await solution.

Let us now suppose that we have got our democratic society, with its right way of living and its basic culture of pots and pans. How then do we procced to build on this foundation?

Culture is a natural growth. If a society has a plenitude of freedom and all the economic essentials of a democratic way of life, then culture will be added without any excessive striving after it. It will come as naturally as the fruit to the well-planted tree. But when I describe the tree as 'well-planted', I am perhaps implying more than a good soil and a sheltered position—the conditions that correspond to the political and economic provi- sions of a natural society. I am perhaps implying a gardener to look after the tree, to safeguard it from pests, to prune away the growth when it is too crowded, to cut out the dead wood. I am. The wild fruit-tree is not to be despised: it is a pretty thing to look at, and it is the healthy stock from which all our garden trees have been cultivated. But cultivation is the distinctive power of man, the power which has enabled him to progress from the animal and the savage state. In his progress man has cultivated, not only animals and plants, but also his own kind. Education is nothing other than self-cultivation, and cultivation, when man directs it to his own species, naturally includes the cultivation of those senses and faculties by means of which man gives form and shape to the things he makes.

I cannot deal adequately with this aspect of my subject without going into the whole question of education in a democratic society, and that subject I have dealt with in another book.[3] But I must state my point of view, because it is fundamental. Briefly, then, I cannot conceive education as a training in so many separate subjects. Education is integral: it is the encouragement of the growth of the whole man, the complete man. It follows that it is not entirely, nor even mainly, an affair of book learning, for that is only the education of one part of our nature—the part of the mind that deals with concepts and abstractions. In the child, who is not yet mature enough to think by these short-cut methods, it should be largely an education of the senses—the senses of sight, touch and hearing: in one word, the education of the *sensibility*. From this point of view there is no valid distinction between art and science: there is only the whole man with his diverse interests and faculties, and the aim of education should be to develop all these in harmony and completeness.

It was Rousseau who first realized this truth, and since Rousseau's time there have been several great educationalists— Froebel, Montessori, Dalcroze, Dewey—who have worked out

[3] *Education Through Art* (London: Faber & Faber, 1943; new edn, 1958).

the practical methods of such an education of the sensibility. It is significant that the last of these, John Dewey, has been led to the conclusion that there is an intimate connection between the right kind of education and a democratic society. You can't have a good educational system except in a democracy—only a democracy guarantees the essential freedom. Equally, you can't have a real democracy without a true system of education; for only by education can a society teach that respect for natural law which is the basis of democracy.

'I cannot repeat too often that it is only objects which can be perceived by the senses which can have any interest for children, especially children whose vanity has not been stimulated nor their minds corrupted by social conventions.' This observation of Rousseau's should be the foundation of our educational methods. A child learns through its senses, and its senses are stimulated by objects—first by natural objects, and then by objects which are the creation of man. Elementary education should teach children how to use their senses—how to see, to touch, to listen—it is far from easy to learn the full and exact use of these faculties. Then, having learned how to use the senses, separately and conjointly, the child should learn how to apply his knowledge: how to judge and compare the true reports that are rendered by his senses; how to construct things that give a true sensuous response and, finally, how to construct things that express his growing awareness of the world and its potentialities.

If we return to our pot and think of the delicate balance of the senses of sight and touch which must guide the potter as the clay turns between his finger-tips, we get some idea of the individual factors involved in all creative activity. If we then remember that the potter must direct the work of his senses towards some useful end—for the pot must function—we get some idea of the social factor involved in all creative activity. Substitute for the potter and his clay any worker and his material, and you are at the heart of all cultural activity: the same conditions persist, from the pot to the poem, from the cottage to the cathedral, from the horseshoe to the aero-engine. Sensibility is the secret of success.

There are degrees of sensibility, just as there are degrees of skill, and education cannot, and should not, smooth them out. But I do not think a democratic society should unduly honour the possessor of exceptional sensibility. It is a gift he owes to the chances of birth, and the possibility of exercising his gift, he owes to the society in which he lives. So much of the world's great art is anonymous, and is none the worse, or none the less appreciated, for the fact. Art always aspires to the impersonal. When every man is an artist, who shall claim to be a superman? Which is only a modern version of the oldest and best of democratic slogans: When Adam delved and Eve span, who was then the gentleman?

When once a democratic society is established, it will inevitably lead to the creation of new values in art, literature, music and science. In some distant time men will call these new values the Democratic Civilization, or the Culture of Democracy, and I believe it will be the greatest and most permanent culture ever created by man. It will have the universal values which we associate with the greatest names in the culture of the past—the universality of Æschylus, Dante and Shakespeare; and it will have these values in a less obscure and a less imperfect form. Æschylus and Dante and Shakespeare are immortal, but they addressed themselves to imperfect societies: to societies still full of moral cruelty, social injustice and perverse superstitions; their works are 'poisonous to the idea of the pride and dignity of the common people, the life-blood of democracy'. The limitations of their audiences hindered, in however small degree, the expression of their vision. A perfect society will not necessarily produce perfect works of art; but in so far as it does produce works of art, the very fact that the artist is appealing to a more highly developed form of society will induce a higher degree of perfection. The artist has a more perfect instrument on which to play.

We should not be discouraged by the fact that all hitherto consciously democratic art has suffered from having to be produced within the framework of a capitalist society. Hitherto not only has the democratic artist had to compromise with the means of communication open to him as a member of a capitalist order—the Press, the cinema, the theatre, etc.—but he has had to use the human material and dramatic situations incidental to that order of society. His only alternative has been to stand self-consciously aside, limiting himself to 'workers' and their experiences—all of which explains the dreariness and monotony of most so-called 'proletarian art'. The artist cannot restrict himself to sectional interests of this kind without detriment to his art: he is only 'all out' and capable of his greatest range when the society he works for is integral, and as wide and varied as humanity itself. It is only in so far as he is simply 'human' that he is wholly 'great'; and it is only in a democratic society that the artist can address humanity and society in the same terms.

To this general rule we must admit certain rare exceptions. Certain types of art are 'archetypal'. That is to say, though they may have a limited range—indeed, by the nature of things, must have this limited range—they are formally perfect. A song by Shakespeare or Blake, a melody by Bach or Mozart, a Persian carpet or a Greek vase—such 'forms', in the words of Keats, 'tease us out of thought as doth eternity'. They tease us out of our human preoccupations—the theme of epic and drama and novel—and for a few brief seconds hold us suspended in a timeless existence. Such rare moments are beyond daily reality, supersocial and in a sense superhuman. But in relation to the whole body of what we call 'art', they are but the glittering pinnacles, and below them spreads the solid structure of human ideals, human vision and human insight: the world of passion and of sentiment, of love and labour and brotherhood.

The only person who seems to have escaped the limitations that have inevitably beset artists of the predemocratic eras is a poet who, in spite of his evident weaknesses, is a prototype or forerunner of the democratic artist—I mean Walt Whitman. The nineteenth-century America in which he lived was by no means a perfect democracy; but the early Americans, especially Jefferson and Lincoln, had had a clear vision of the requisites of a democratic society, and they inspired Whitman with the ambition to be the first poet of this new order. He was fired by a realization of the tremendous potentialities of the New World into which he had been born:

'Sole among nationalities, these States have assumed the task to put in forms of lasting power and practicality, on areas of amplitude rivalling the operations of the physical kosmos, the moral political speculations of ages, long, long deferr'd, the democratic republican principle, and the theory of development and perfection by voluntary standards, and self-reliance.'

But these potentialities could never be realized on the political plane alone:

'I say that democracy can never prove itself beyond cavil, until it founds and luxuriantly grows its own forms of art, poems, schools, theology, displacing all that exists, or that has been produced anywhere in the past, under opposite influences.'

'The priest departs, the divine literatus comes.' In these words Walt Whitman sums up the whole argument of this essay. But let the reader turn to Democratic Vistas, that credo of Walt Whitman's from which my quotations come, and let him find there in fullness the essential democratic truths, and in particular those that relate to the enduring values of human life, and to their expression in enduring works of art. And from this prose work of the good grey poet let the reader turn to *Leaves of Grass* and see if he does not find there, shining through the crudities and contradictions which Whitman himself was the first to admit, the lineaments of our divine literatus, our democratic poet and exemplar. Such may not be the form of the art of the future, but it is its prophetic spirit—

'Expanding and swift, henceforth,
Elements, breeds, adjustments, turbulent, quick and
audacious,
A world primal again, vistas of glory incessant and branching,
A new race dominating previous ones and grander far, with
new contests,
New politics, new literature and religions, new inventions and
arts.

These, my voice announcing—I will sleep no more but arise,
You oceans that have been calm within me! how I feel you,
fathomless, stirring, preparing unprecedented waves and
storms.'

3

THE POLITICS OF THE UNPOLITICAL

If certain writers feel emancipated enough from all that is human—they would say *intellectual* enough—to continue to fulfil, under any circumstances whatever, the strange functions of purely abstract thought, good luck to them. But those who can only conceive their role as writers to be a means of experiencing more deeply and of establishing more fully a mode of existence which they want to be human, those who only *write* in order to feel themselves *living* integrally—such people no longer have the right to be disinterested. The trend of events, and the evolution of ideas, if they run out their course, will lead straight to an unparalleled deformation of the individual human being. Whoever gazes into the future which is being forged for us, and can there perceive the monstrous and denatured brother whom one will necessarily resemble, cannot react except by a revolt into extreme egoism. It is this egoism which must now be rehabilitated. Today the problem of the person effaces all others. The intelligence is placed in such circumstances that for it disinterestedness and resignation come to the same thing.

Thierry Maulnier, *La Crise est dans l'homme* (Paris, 1932).

The politics of the unpolitical—these are the politics of those who desire to be pure in heart: the politics of men without personal ambition; of those who have not desired wealth or an unequal share of worldly possessions; of those who have always striven, whatever their race or condition, for human values and not for national or sectional interests.

For our Western world, Christ is the supreme example of this unselfish devotion to the good of humanity, and the Sermon on the Mount is the source of all the politics of the unpolitical. But others who came before Christ and who may have influenced him elaborated their political ideals in pureness of heart—Lao-Tzu and Zeno, for example; and among Christ's direct disciples we must include several philosophers and prophets nearer to our time, whose message is still insistent and directly applicable to our present condition—Ruskin and Kropotkin, Morris and Tolstoy, Gandhi and Eric Gill. These modern representatives of what we might well call an ancient tradition form a closely inter-related body of thought: Gandhi, for example, declared his debt to Ruskin and Tolstoy; Gill was a disciple of Morris, who was himself a disciple of Ruskin; Kropotkin was closely associated with Morris. Ruskin, in this succession, has a certain pre-eminence and originality: the vitality and transforming power[1] of his writings seem to come straight from his deep study of the Bible and from his prolonged meditation on the words of Christ; though he had in himself that rare power which Gandhi recognized as the specifically poetic power—his power 'to call forth the good latent in the human breast'. We are still far from estimating the full extent of this great man's influence, but we can describe it as ethical and aesthetic rather than as religious or political. Ruskin's eloquence did not bring into being either a

---

[1] 'The one book that brought about an instantaneous and practical transformation in my life was *Unto this Last*.'—*Mahatma Gandhi: His Own Story* (London, 1930), p. 163.

new sect or a new party; his power is emotive and not calcula-
tive, and in this as in other respects he is nearly related to Rousseau, having for our own revolutionary period almost exactly the
same significance as Rousseau had for the French Revolutionary
period. We may still come to regard *Unto this Last* as the *Contrat
Social* of a new society—as the Manifesto of those communists
who renounce political action in their efforts to establish a new
society.

Of the six names mentioned, Morris was the only one who
compromised on this political issue, but he never, to the end of
his life, reconciled himself to the political methods advocated by
his friends. His lecture on 'The Policy of Abstention' (1887) is
the best statement of the case against parliamentary action ever
made in English, and it is a pity that it is so entirely forgotten by
socialists today, and that it is only available in a limited and
expensive publication.[2] Towards the end of his life Gandhi also,
it might be said, made a tactical compromise of some kind with
the politically minded leaders of the Congress Party. He worked
in close association with them, but always in a relationship
which he himself has described as 'experimental'. For the whole
of Gandhi's life and teaching were directed against parliamentary action: the doctrine of *ahimsa*, or non-violence, rejected
the violence of majority government no less decisively than the
violence of military oppression. In the end his methods met
with complete success.

It is characteristic of these six teachers that although they
would be included among the most revolutionary figures of the
past hundred years, we do not spontaneously associate the word
'democracy' with any of them. Democracy is a very ambiguous
word, and its meanings vary from a sentimental sympathy for
the poor and oppressed such as we get in Christian Socialism, to

[2] *William Morris: Artist, Writer, Socialist*, by May Morris (2 vols. Oxford: Basil
Blackwell, 1936), vol. ii. pp. 434–53.

a ruthless dogma of proletarian dictatorship such as we have seen established in Russia. Our Six were all democrats in the former sense; none of them was a democrat in the latter sense. But it is an important distinction, and if in the name of democracy we are more and more inevitably compelled to commit ourselves to the political machinery of the state—to the nationalization of industry, to the bureaucratic control of all spheres of life and to the doctrine of the infallibility of the People (divinely invested in a unique Party)—then it is time to renounce the democratic label and seek a less equivocal name. My use of the word 'democracy' is always subject to this consideration.

A complete renunciation of the word is not easy: indeed, it has been deliberately made difficult for us, not only by the common usage of many ardent seekers after the truth, but also by the deliberate propaganda of the enemies of liberty. A common form of this Machiavellian sophistry consists in presenting your opponent with an apparently inescapable alternative—an 'either/or' which you accept as covering all the known facts. In our own time, in the sphere of world politics, this either/or is *either* democracy *or* fascism. Such an alternative seems to leave communism out of account, but not in reality. If you question people about the relation of communism to democracy, the communists among them will tell you that communism is the extreme form of democracy, and the anti-communists will say that communism as it exists in Russia is merely another form of totalitarianism.

Both these views are right. Communism is an extreme form of democracy, and it is totalitarian: but equally the totalitarian state in the form of fascism is an extreme form of democracy. All forms of socialism, whether state socialism of the Russian kind, or national socialism of the German kind, or democratic socialism of the British kind, are professedly democratic: that is to say, they all obtain popular assent by the manipulation of mass psychology. All are actually majority governments.

The weaknesses of democracy have been exposed by every political philosopher since Plato and Aristotle. Even Rousseau, the so-called Father of Democracy, rejected it as a system practicable for any society larger than a city state. The philosophers, being men of intelligence, have never been able to suggest anything better than a dictatorship of the intelligentsia; but knowing how unlikely it is that such a dictatorship would be long tolerated by the ignorant masses, they have tried to disguise the inevitability of some alternative form of dictatorship under a picturesque formula. Historically the most effective of these is constitutional monarchy. It has always been recognized that a king might easily degenerate into a tyrant, but his natural life is limited and can at a pinch be artificially shortened; whereas the reign of an aristocracy, which is the next best possibility, has no mensurable limit: it can only be brought to an end by a civil war with all its miseries.

The plain fact about democracy is that it is a physical impossibility. In an aggregation of millions of individuals such as we always have in modern society, we may get government of the people and even government for the people, but never for a moment government by the people. But that is the essential test, for if a people does not govern itself, it is governed by somebody else; *ipso facto* it is no longer a democracy. This is not merely a logical quibble: democracy never has in fact existed in modern times. In our own country, for example, the monarchical system was overthrown by an oligarchy, and since the 'Great' Revolution of 1688 we have been governed by a succession of oligarchies, which might be Whig or might be Tory, might represent the landed interests or the moneyed interests, but never for a moment represented the people as a whole. In our own time a new oligarchy, the oligarchy of the trade unions, as exclusive a caste as ever aspired to power, has competed, luckily in vain, for the control of the state. It is now openly merging itself with the ascendant oligarchy of monopoly capitalism, to form what James Burnham has called 'the managerial class'.

All this is such an obvious interpretation of the historical facts that no one but a fool can deceive himself in the belief that democracy has ever been, or is ever likely to be, a reality in a modern industrial community. A constitutional monarchy as a cloak for competing sectional interests, as a symbol of unity in a society which would otherwise disintegrate from ruthless class warfare—that is the definition of the British constitution. The French Republic, the United States of America, the German and Italian Republics are all constitutions of the same character: they only differ in nomenclature and the trimming on their uniforms.

Nevertheless this must be said (if only in justification of the lip service which so many of us have paid to democracy at various times): the political doctrine known as democracy has implied an important principle which, if it were not systematically misinterpreted and misunderstood, would still justify us in using the word. This is the *principle of equality*—an ethical doctrine, even a religious dogma. The equality of man implies many things, but never its literal meaning. No one believes that all men are equal in capacity or talent: they are in fact outrageously diverse. But nevertheless, in Christian phraseology, they are all equal in the sight of God; and to affirm our common humanity is the first article of freedom. Whatever government we establish, whatever way of life we follow, all our faith is built on error unless we respect the rights of the person—that is to say, his right to be a person, a unique entity, 'human left, from human free'.

This is the fundamental doctrine of a Christian community and of all other types of essential communism. It is even fundamental to the communism of Marx and Engels. But the equality acknowledged by democracy has in practice been something very different. God has been eliminated from the formula and we are left with a mere equalization or levelling of man with man. The spiritual measure has been discarded, and man is left to dangle in material scales; and for centuries the counter-weight has been a piece of silver. The only way in which democracy has been able to assess equality is in terms of money, and it is the inability of the trade union movement, especially in Great Britain and Germany, to break away from this cash valuation of humanity which has, more than any other single factor, made the democratic working-class movement a futile diversion of revolutionary effort.[3]

By what values a man shall be judged absolutely we will not discuss here, but socially, as a man among his fellow-men, he should be judged by his creative ability, by his power to add to the common stock of goods. The value of a man is the value of the art he practises—whether it is the art of healing or the art of making music, the art of road-mending or the art of cooking. We might place first of all the art of making children, because on that the continuance of the human race depends. Procreation is perhaps the only art which is literally creative: the rest of the arts are merely inventive.

For this and for reasons more strictly sociological, our social philosophy must begin with the family. From whatever realistic angle we approach the problems of human life, the family is seen as the integral unit, without which there is no social organization, no social progress, no social order or human happiness. But

[3] Chiefly because it has prevented the workers from concentrating on the enhancement of their human dignity by the acquisition of responsibility for the direction and control of industry. But also because, as Franz Borkenau has shown so effectively, it has prevented the development of international solidarity among the workers, for the wage-rate is directly dependent on the international market, not only of labour, but of commodities. For this reason the workers have been forced to realize that their interests are bound up, not only with the interests of their employers, but also with the competitive expansion of the national economy. Cf. F. Borkenau, *Socialism, National or International* (Routledge, 1942).

we must insist that this is a sociological problem, and we must dissociate ourselves from those who think it can be solved by moral persuasion. Families are encouraged and sustained by security of life and property, decent housing, and an environment in which nurture and education can be natural and serene. Morality and religion may give their sanction to the social unit thus established: it is the fascist way of thinking to imagine that such sanctions are a substitute for economic action.

The next essential group is the guild—the association of men and women according to their calling or practical function. (I obstinately retain the word 'guild', in spite of its medieval and sentimental associations, because it is more human, and euphonious, than such expressions as 'collective', 'co-operative', 'soviet', etc.) The guild is a vertical and not a horizontal organization: it includes all persons associated together in the production of a particular commodity. The agricultural guild, for example, would include the drivers and mechanics who run the tractors: the engineers' guild would include the men who make the tractors. But the vertical organization will be divided into regional and district units, and the main business of the guilds will always take place in the district units; decisions will arise out of personal contacts and not from the abstract and legalistic conclaves of a central bureau.

Decentralization is thus also of the essence of this alternative to democracy. 'Real politics are local politics', and power and authority should be devolved and segmented to the utmost limit of practicability. Only in such a way can the person—every person in society—be assured of an adequate sense of responsibility and human dignity. These qualities for the average person only emerge in his actual sphere of work and in his regional environment.

The trend to centralization is a disease of democracy, and not, as is so often assumed, of the machine. It arises inevitably from the concentration of power in parliament, from the separation

made between responsibility and creative activity, from the
massing of production for greater profits and higher wages. The
evolution of democracy is parallel to the growth of centralization, and centralization is in no sense an inevitable process.
Modern warfare has revealed its extraordinary inefficiency. The
guerrillas of Jugoslavia showed more initiative than the bureaucrats of London or Berlin. The centralization of control in a
democratic state is clumsy, inhuman and inert. Incapable of
thought, originality or enterprise, it can only act under the dictatorship of a Hitler or a Churchill—even the shrill voices of an
exasperated Press have no effect on it.

The health and happiness of society depend on the labour and
science of its members; but neither health nor happiness is possible unless that work and science are directed and controlled by
the workers themselves. A guild is by definition autonomous
and self-governing. Every man who is a master of his craft
acquires thereby the right to a voice in the direction of his
workshop. He also acquires security of tenure and of income.
Indeed, his income and his tenure should depend on his qualifications rather than on the tally of his labours. He should begin
to receive an income from the moment he has chosen a calling
and been admitted as an apprentice of a trade or profession—
which will be long before he has left school. His income will
rise with his qualifications, and will depend entirely on his
qualifications. Any rational society will naturally make use of the
services of a qualified worker, because it thereby increases the
general well-being. If it fails to do so, that society is restricting
production; and if such restriction is in the general interest,
then society should pay the worker for his qualifications until
they can be used, or otherwise pay the worker to train and
acquire more immediately useful qualifications. The talents and
acquired skill of a person are his property: his contribution to
the common wealth. Society should be organized to secure the
maximum utilization of its inherent wealth, and the productive

organizations themselves will then decide how this common wealth is best increased—by machinery or handicraft, by large factories or small workshops, in towns or villages. The human values involved, and not an abstract and numerical profit, will be the criterion.

Education, in such a society, is initiation. It is the revelation of innate capacities, the training of these capacities in socially useful activities, the disciplining of these activities to aesthetic and moral ends.

Such a natural organization of society leaves little activity to the state as such. The state remains merely as the arbiter, to decide in the interests of the whole the conflicts which emerge in the parts. Such a function is already exercised by an independent judiciary, which might well extend its functions to cover the rights of the citizen as consumer. An Economic Council, constituted by much the same means as the Bench, would be necessary to safeguard society as a whole against a policy of restrictionism in any particular guild, to direct the general volume of production and to maintain a balanced output among its tributary guilds. It is difficult to see the necessity for any other central authority.

All this may seem to amount to a programme far more definite and dogmatic than the title of my essay promised, but to be unpolitical does not mean to be without politics: every attitude that is more than egoistic is to that extent social, and a social attitude is a political attitude. But it is one thing to have politics, and another thing to pursue them. It is one thing to have a faith, and another thing to trade on the credulity of the faithful. It is not the substance of politics we should object to, but the methods of the politician. We should refuse to invest our private interests in a public policy, for we know that what cannot be won by a change of heart, which is also a revolution of reason, is only won by cheats and impostors.

Let me summarize the essential features of a natural society:

   I. The liberty of the person.
  II. The integrity of the family.
 III. The reward of qualifications.
 IV. The self-government of the guilds.
  V. The abolition of parliament and centralized government.
 VI. The institution of arbitrament.
VII. The delegation of authority.
VIII. The humanization of industry.

The social order thus envisaged is international because it is essentially pacific: it is pacific because it is essentially international. It aims at the production of world-wide plenty, at the humanization of work, and at the eradication of all economic conflicts. It may be, as some philosophers hold, that an aggressive instinct is innate in man, and that no organization of society can guard against its expression. In that case the world can only be made tolerable in the degree that this instinct can be controlled by reason. Reason has no chance if men are starving, or even if they have undue cause for envy. But granted an economy that is no longer competitive, in which the highest yield of production is wisely and evenly distributed among all mankind, then reason will have a chance. Instincts are not immutable: they can be transformed, sublimated, diverted into creative channels. Energy itself is not evil: it only becomes evil by being applied to evil ends.

4

THE CULT OF LEADERSHIP

I am against bigness and greatness in all their forms, and with the invisible molecular moral forces that work from individual to individual, stealing in through the crannies of the world like so many soft rootlets, or like the capillary oozing of water, and yet rending the hardest monuments of man's pride, if you give them time. The bigger the unit you deal with, the hollower, the more brutal, the more mendacious is the life displayed. So I am against all big organizations as such, national ones first and foremost; against all big successes and big results; and in favour of the eternal forces of truth which always work in the individual and immediately unsuccessful way, underdogs always, till history comes, after they are long dead, and puts them on the top.

William James, *Letters*, II, 90.

In more than one of these essays I am concerned to show that from a certain point of view there is nothing to choose between fascism and democracy—that the economic and military antagonisms inherent in modern civilization involve both fascism and democracy alike and constitute irrecoverable encroachments on the physical and spiritual liberty of the person. The incursions of democracy are far more dangerous because they are far more deceitful. They are always accompanied by a smoke-screen of righteousness which hides their real nature and dimensions, even from many who are most salient in the attack. The very preamble of this menacing strategy is the cult of leadership, for this cult is essentially the denial of that principle of equality upon which alone a community of free individuals can be established.

Fascism is a complex social phenomenon for which there is no single or simple explanation. It is obviously not a national phenomenon—it triumphed in Latin Italy no less successfully than in Nordic Germany, and some of its symptoms have been diagnosed in this country and the United States of America. I do not think it is worth wasting any time on the proposition that fascism was the inevitable development of certain historical trends in Germany. Germany was the weakest spot in the body of world politics, and for that reason it was most easily and most successfully infected by the disease. That weakness in the political structure of Germany can be explained historically, and German philosophers have quite naturally tended to find elaborate justifications for it. But if a disease like cancer attacks, say, the liver, it is quite unscientific to say that the liver is the cause of the cancer. Cancer is a disease of the whole body which may become manifest in the liver or any other 'weak spot'.

I do not wish to dismiss the historical origins of fascism as of no importance: they do explain why the disease should develop in one nation rather than in another. History investigates the organic tissue of society just as histology investigates the organic tissue of the human body. History is always *post mortem*—it can tell us *why* this happened *here*. But it cannot explain the processes governing the immediate emotions of the collective organisms we call states or nations. The only science that can attempt such an explanation is psychology.

It will be said that I have forgotten economics. Marxians in particular will be eager to point out that I have forgotten my dialectical materialism, but I would claim to have remembered my dialectics as well as my materialism. There is no doubt that economic factors played an enormous part in the growth of fascism. Hitler himself was fond of tracing the origins of his success to the injustices of the Versailles Treaty, which was an undisguised expression of economic forces. He was not so fond of admitting what is equally true, that he was helped to power by certain groups of capitalists. If Hitler consciously represented any economic interest, it was that of the 'little man', the bankrupt shopkeeper, the small capitalist who had been put out of business by the big monopolies and chain stores.[1] But even this sympathy was not genuine.

The economic origins of fascism have been traced by more than one writer. In the period after the First World War it was the middle class, and particularly the *lower* middle class, that found itself threatened by the sudden growth of monopolist capitalism. It developed an acute state of anxiety, even of panic: a psychological neurosis which led to a craving for leadership and a craving for submission. It was of this state of mind, this disease of the spirit, that Hitler took advantage. It is a development in mass psychology which has been very acutely analysed by Erich Fromm in *The Fear of Freedom*.[2] According to Dr. Fromm, Hitler succeeded so well because he was able to combine the qualities of a resentful petty-bourgeois, with whom the middle classes could identify themselves, emotionally and socially, with those of an opportunist ready to serve the interests of the German industrialists and Junkers.

This is not the place, nor would I at any time feel competent,

[1] 'We want our middle class, which is becoming poorer and poorer and whose means of livelihood are cut off more and more by large business concerns, to be placed in a position where they can have their share in these goods.'—Hitler in an interview with a representative of the Associated Press, 1932.

[2] London (Kegan Paul), 1942. Title in U.S.A. *Escape from Freedom*.

to undertake an analysis of the economic principles of the National Socialist movement. Some people—Dr. Fromm, for example—believe that such principles did not exist; that the only principle professed by the Nazis was a radical opportunism. I think this is a dangerous simplification. It is true that fascism is not basically an expression of economic forces: to accept that view would be to accept the Marxist interpretation of history, and never for a moment, in theory or in practice, did Hitler do that. His movement was an attempt to deny this principle, and to put in its place a principle of the particular endowment of races, and in the final analysis of individuals within the race. Achievement is the result of specific genius or capacity and not of blind forces. Let me quote a key passage from one of Hitler's own speeches:

'The greatness of a people is the result not of the sum of all its achievements but in the last resort of the sum of its outstanding achievements. Let no one say that the picture produced as a first impression of human civilization is the impression of its achievement as a whole. This whole edifice of civilization is in its foundations and in all its stones nothing else than the result of the creative capacity, the achievement, the intelligence, the industry of individuals: in its greatest triumphs it represents the great crowning achievement of individual god-favoured geniuses, in its average accomplishment the achievement of men of average capacity, and in its sum doubtless the result of the use of human labour-force in order to turn to account the creations of genius and of talent. So it is only natural that when the capable intelligences of a nation, which are always in a minority, are regarded as only of the same value as all the rest, then genius, capacity, the value of personality are slowly subjected to the majority, and this process is then falsely named the rule of the people. For this is not the rule of the people, but in reality the rule of stupidity, of mediocrity, of half-heartedness, of cowardice, of weakness, and of inadequacy. Rule of the people means rather that a people should allow itself to be governed and led by its most capable individuals, those who are born to the task, and not that a chance majority which of necessity is alien to these tasks should be permitted to administer all spheres of life.'[3]

This is a classic formulation of the doctrine of leadership. In effect it is the doctrine of power politics, and power politics have always shown an extreme contempt for economics and even for reason. Civilization may owe its highest achievements to individual god-favoured geniuses, but there has always been something haphazard in their incidence, and it is also true that civilization owes its darkest hours to evil geniuses who have been equally individual. A secure civilization cannot be based on such a gamble, and it is only individuals who hope to benefit from such a gamble who erect it into a historical principle. In this way they hope to disguise their naked craving for power, which is the fundamental factor in all their thoughts and actions. This craving for power is an irrational force—it can no more be explained by economic factors than a craving for drink or for drugs, though, like these cravings, it can be encouraged or thwarted by economic factors.

The necessary analysis of that craving for power, which is the basic factor in the psychology of fascism, has been done, most convincingly in my opinion, by the writer just quoted, Dr. Fromm. Any such analysis involves the use of more technical terms than are justified in the present context, but let me try to summarize Dr Fromm's argument very briefly. It begins dialectically enough with economic and historical factors—with the

---

[3] From a speech delivered to the Industry Club in Düsseldorf, 27th January 1932. From *The Speeches of Adolf Hitler*, trans. by Norman H. Baynes (Oxford, 1942), vol. i. pp. 784–5.

historical struggle of man to gain freedom from the political, economic and spiritual shackles which bound him through long centuries of darkness and despair. It shows that time after time man has been afraid to use the freedom he has gained, and has fallen back on some alternative system of control. He has submissively held up his wrists to a new gaoler—some new authoritarian religion, like Calvinism; some new economic tyranny, like capitalism. The individual, it seems, is afraid to be alone. 'To feel completely alone and isolated leads to mental disintegration, just as physical starvation leads to death.' The individual craves for relatedness, for union and, Fromm points out, 'even being related to the basest kind of pattern is immensely preferable to being alone. Religion and nationalism, as well as any custom and any belief, however absurd and degrading, if it only connects the individual with others, are refuges from what man most dreads: isolation.' Dr. Fromm then quotes a very effective passage from Balzac:

> 'But learn one thing, impress it upon your mind which is still so malleable: man has a horror of aloneness. And of all kinds of aloneness, moral aloneness is the most terrible. The first hermits lived with God. They inhabited the world which is most populated, the world of the spirits. The first thought of man, be he a leper or a prisoner, a sinner or an invalid, is: to have a companion of his fate. In order to satisfy this drive which is life itself, he applies all his strength, all his power, the energy of his whole life.'[4]

The true solution of this problem implies communism, but communism in the original sense of the word, as used by anarchists, and not in the sense used by Marxians and their opponents. I mean communism conceived as a spontaneous

[4] Op. cit., pp. 15–16.

association of individuals for mutual aid. But lacking this rational conception, man has only been able to get rid of his isolation by desperate means—by those psychological obsessions which we call sadism and masochism. Sadism is the unconscious impulse to acquire unrestricted power over another person, and to test the fullness of his power by destroying that other person. Masochism is the unconscious impulse to dissolve oneself in the power of another person and to participate in his annihilating power. Fascism is the combined expression of these two unconscious impulses—its peculiarity resides in this ambivalence, this continual shifting from one impulse to the other, from sadistic destructiveness to masochistic submissiveness.

There is no need to illustrate these characteristics from the behaviour of the fascist parties in Germany and Italy: that has been done in hundreds of books, and Hitler's own book, *Mein Kampf*, is at once a case-book and a text-book of these psychological aberrations. The Nazi leaders were driven by an overwhelming lust for power—that fact needs no demonstration. The Nazi followers were driven by an equally overwhelming lust to surrender themselves to this power.

Fromm's thesis, then, is that these sadistic and masochistic trends in modern history explain the inability of the isolated individual to stand alone, to make use of the freedom he has gained. Accepting this as a convincing explanation of the psychological forces underlying fascism, let us now consider whether there do not exist among us certain tendencies of the same nature—tendencies which, if not checked, will inevitably lead to fascism.

The most prevalent manifestation of these latent tendencies is the universal demand for leadership, a demand which, not only by implication, but even in expression, is identical with the Nazi doctrine. Schools are urged to train boys for 'the tasks of leadership', students are asked to develop the qualities of leadership, selection boards make these same qualities the criterion of their choice of candidates for commissions in the army, navy and air force. Even workers are urged to select their leaders—their shop stewards and shift leaders. In the political sphere we have adopted the *Führerprinzip* without qualification.

Before we examine what is involved in this general desire for leadership, let us distinguish a quality which is often confused with leadership, and is perhaps always incorporated in it. I mean the quality of individual initiative. This is fundamentally the impulse to originate, to construct, and, in relation to other individuals, the desire to distinguish oneself. It is a self-expressive impulse, and has nothing in common with the will to power.

Now this realization of the self—the expression of the uniqueness of the individual—is, as I shall emphasize presently, one of the most essential features of an organic community, and must be preserved at all costs. But the individual can only realize himself in the community; or rather, the difference between realizing oneself in the community and realizing oneself in *spite* of the community is precisely the distinction I want to make. In the one case, the uniqueness of the individual becomes part of the pattern of society; in the other case, the individual remains outside the pattern, an unassimilated and therefore essentially neurotic element.

What I think emerges from these considerations is that the failure of democracy to realize an integrated pattern of society is largely due to its reliance on leaders. Through generations we have spent our blood and expended our utmost efforts on getting rid of the leadership of priests and kings, aristocrats and captains of industry, only to find that it has all been futile, only to find ourselves with the same infantile longing to be led. We talk about the brotherhood of man, about comradeship and cooperation, and these phrases do describe the deepest instincts of humanity; but in actual fact we are children seeking a father, brothers and sisters full of mutual jealousy and suspicion, repeating on a national scale the neurotic conflicts of the family.

It may be argued that, however beautiful they may be as ideals, brotherhood, comradeship and co-operation are impracticable modes of conducting the business of a state in peace and war—especially in war. We are told that in war we must have discipline, and discipline implies command and obedience, commanders and obeyers, officers and privates. But the falseness of that assumption has been clearly demonstrated. It was clearly demonstrated in the two world wars, though victory had the unfortunate effect of making it unnecessary for us to learn the lessons of that conflict. But those lessons, which received a striking confirmation in the Spanish Civil War, were not lost on our enemies, and their successes in Poland, in France, in Greece and everywhere except in Russia, where they came up against an army that had learned the same lesson, is due precisely to what might be called the democratization of the army.[5]

---

[5] The Russian evidence is not unequivocal: cf. General Drassilnikov, in an article quoted by A. Werth in *Moscow*, '41, p. 85: 'Present-day warfare requires such enormous moral tension that only the most firmly disciplined troops can face it, and maintain their fighting powers intact. That is why such drastic steps have had to be taken towards the final liquidation of the pseudo-democratic traditions in the army, traditions which only undermined discipline.' But, according to Werth himself, the situation is now very different: 'Since the war began, and since this article was written, the political commissars have, of course, had their power restored; though not at the expense of the officers. Roughly speaking, the officer is, as before, responsible for the military operations; but the political commissar is the man who is in charge of the troops' morale, and, incidentally, of the officer's morale.' But the commissars were finally abolished by Stalin's decree on 11th October 1942. Commenting on this news, *The Times* special correspondent in Moscow observed:

'When the system of political commissars was introduced, the young Red Army was officered by many men whose loyalty to the revolutionary régime was suspect, and who were only retained in the army because of the shortage of trained officers. Since then, however, the Red Army's military academies have created commanders who are completely identified with the régime and *whose thoughts and language are the same as those of the men they command* [my italics]. There will still be a need for political education in the army. As before, the Red

Several independent witnesses confirmed the genuineness of this process of democratization in the German army. Shirer, for example, in his *Berlin Diary*, reports that:

'Few people who have not seen it in action realize how different this army is from the one the Kaiser sent hurtling into Belgium and France in 1914. . . . The great gulf between officers and men is gone in this war. There is a sort of equalitarianism. I felt it from the first day I came in contact with the army at the front. The German officer no longer represents—or at least is conscious of representing—a class or caste. And the men in the ranks feel this. They feel like members of one great family. Even the salute has a new meaning. German privates salute each other, thus making the gesture more of a comradely greeting than the mere recognition of superior rank. In cafés, restaurants, dining-cars, officers and men off duty sit at the same table and converse as men to men. This would have been unthinkable in the last war and is probably unusual in the

Army man will be told the significance of the operations in which he is playing a part, however small. But the division of duties that was summed up in M. Stalin's phrase of 1919 that the regimental commissar is the father and soul of the regiment, while the commander is its will, will no longer be so precise. The best of the present commissars will become commanders, and all Red Army commanders will have political *aides* subordinate to them.'

On the same date (12th October) *The Times* reported a further development in the German army, designed to remove the final traces of class distinction between the officers and their men:

'According to an announcement by the High Command, candidates for commissioned rank in the German Army need not in future hold a school leaving certificate or have attended a particular type of school.

'The essential qualifications, in addition to "character and pure Aryan blood", are to be "worthiness for army service, readiness to serve Nationalist-Socialist Germany and its Führer, and idealism".

'The German News Agency remarks that this decision follows Hitler's recent declaration that "every man in the National-Socialist army carries a field-marshal's baton in his knapsack".'

armies of the West, including our own. In the field, officers and men usually eat from the same soup kitchen.'[6]

I do not want to enter into an academic discussion of the distinction between discipline and morale. We all know that discipline depends on the exercise of authority: it has been defined as 'the enforced obedience to external authority' and nothing can disguise its bi-polar nature and internal strain. It is sometimes said that if discipline is thoroughly enforced it becomes instinctive, but that is not borne out either by psychological investigations or by military experience. It thus comes about that even while maintaining an undemocratic structure in the army, and an undemocratic structure of society, the present tendency of all governments is to rely on the creation of morale, in the civilian population no less than in the armed forces.

Morale is a group feeling: it is a feeling of cohesion, of unity in the face of danger, and at present it is normally only brought about in conditions of danger, when the group is threatened with extinction. These conditions are brought about, not only by war, but by threats of starvation or subjugation. The morale of a trade union on strike, for example, depends not so much on political consciousness, the ideological struggle for better conditions of work and of life, as on the direct feeling of group solidarity in the face of the insecurity occasioned by the stoppage of work.

What is admirable in the past and desirable for the future is a form of society that succeeds in maintaining morale—as distinct from discipline—under conditions of peace. The feeling of relatedness, of union, which we all experience spontaneously when threatened by invasion, or air raids, or the blockade, should be realized for positive purpose, for the creation of a just

[6] William L. Shirer, *Berlin Diary* (London, 1941), pp. 345–6.

society, a natural way of life. There again I think the fascists seized on an essential psychological truth—and distorted it by using it for their own ends. They realized that a society can only be built up on the principle of association. They therefore had to abolish the existing organizations, because they were pacifist and international—that is to say, essentially diffusionist—and to replace them by new organizations designed to canalize the national spirit. But they realized that this could not be accomplished by coercion. The whole of their educational system, their youth movement, their labour front and their party organization had no other aim but the creation of a spirit stronger than discipline. But the morale thus achieved was not limited to the biological function of group preservation; it was then extended to an ideological function of group expansion, group assertion, group domination. A distortion arose from the fact that the spontaneous origin and organic growth of association was thus obliterated, being replaced by an artificial and superimposed conception of the state, by a new order which was essentially a planned order.

We should always clearly distinguish between the aims and the methods of fascism. The aims are entirely undemocratic, irrational and irresponsible. But some of the methods—by no means all—are more democratic, more psychologically effective, and altogether more successful, than the methods hitherto used by the democracies. Even in this matter of leadership, the Nazis in particular avoided the psychological crudities which we not only attributed to them, but innocently imitate. It seems to me—and I am mainly relying on what Hitler himself has written in *Mein Kampf*, and on his later speeches and personal behaviour—that in their realization of the supreme importance of morale the Nazis adopted a conception of leadership radically different from that entertained in our public schools and military forces. The difference is rather a subtle one, but at least we must give Hitler some credit for subtlety.

In his well-known work on *Psychology and Primitive Culture*, Professor Bartlett discusses the relationship of the chief to the primitive group, and points out that:

> 'it is a relationship in which leadership does not depend mainly upon domination or assertion, but upon a ready susceptibility to the thoughts, feelings and actions of the members of the group. The chief, that is, *expresses* the group rather than *impresses* it. This is a kind of relationship, entirely different, it seems to me, from dominance and assertiveness. . . .'

'A ready susceptibility to the thoughts, feelings and actions of the members of the group'—this phrase might be taken as an apt description of the very quality which Hitler claims to possess.[7] No unprejudiced observer of his career can deny Hitler a certain representative character—though we must

---

[7] 'Owing to the peculiar circumstances of my life, I am perhaps more capable than anyone else of understanding and realizing the nature and the whole life of the various German castes. Not because I have been able to look down on this life from above but because I have participated in it, because I stood in the midst of this life, because Fate, in a moment of caprice or perhaps fulfilling the designs of Providence, cast me into the great mass of the people, among common folk. Because I myself was a labouring man for years in the building trade and had to earn my own bread. And because for a second time I took my place once again as an ordinary soldier amongst the masses, and because then life raised me into other strata (*Schichten*) of our own people, so that I know these, too, better than countless others who were born in these strata. So Fate has perhaps fitted me more than any other to be the broker—I think I may say the honest broker—for both sides alike' (Speech of 10th May 1933: op cit., vol. i. p. 862). It is this pose of 'honest broker' which distinguishes Hitler from most of the leaders of the past and all those of the present. The democratic leaders (Churchill, Roosevelt) generally come from the upper strata, but if they do come from the same level as Hitler (Ramsay MacDonald, for example) they either make a virtue of their origins or despise them. Hitler is unique, I think, in trying to maintain this pose of 'an independent man'.

remember that a demagogue will always begin by creating the dissatisfaction which he then sets out to exploit. He earns his easiest honours by alleviating imaginary ills. But it is no ordinary faculty which enables a man to do that. Again let me emphasize that we are concerned with an instrument and not with the use to which it is put. Intuition, to use for the moment the term Hitler himself used to favour—intuition may be an admirable quality in a rational human being, a beneficent aid to the poet, and scientist and the engineer; but the same quality combined with a sadistic craving for power becomes a destructive force.

I repeat, therefore, that we must not underestimate the *methods*, as opposed to the *motives* of fascism. The motives are the individual lust for power and the racial lust for world domination; but the methods, which include war, persecution, brutality and bestiality of all kinds, also include the establishment of group unity and devotion to a common ideal—features which we assume are essentially democratic. 'If', says Hitler towards the end of *Mein Kampf*, 'if in its historical development the German people had possessed this group unity as it was enjoyed by other peoples, then the German Reich would today probably be mistress of the globe'. And he says elsewhere in the same book that with the Aryan the instinct for self-preservation had reached its noblest form 'because he willingly subjects his own ego to the life of the community, and, if the hour should require it, he also sacrifices it'.

If only, one cannot help thinking, such a feeling for unity and self-sacrifice could have been devoted to something nobler than the conquest of individual power and racial domination. But that is to ignore the reality of the neurosis from which the lust for power springs. The extraordinary success of Hitler was due to the fact that his sado-masochistic impulses, which are explained by his personal history—the frustrated artist, divorced from his own class and rejected by the class he aspired to, the typical isolated, declassed individual in whom the sadistic neurosis develops most strongly—the extraordinary success of such an individual was due to the fact that his personal neurosis is representative of the collective neurosis of a nation which has also been frustrated in its desire for expansion, its desire for a superior position in the society of nations. In their masochistic longings such a people will eagerly submit to the absolute power of a leader and will only require one liberty in return—the liberty to satisfy the sadistic side of their neurosis by the persecution of some minority, some degraded class. Hence the important part played by anti-Semitism in the evolution of German fascism.

I hope I have shown that a dangerous ambiguity lurks in this cry for leadership, this reliance on a popular leader, which characterizes democratic no less than fascist communities in time of war. It is, I believe, not merely a sign of weakness, a sign of war-weariness: it is positively the symptom of a latent state of fascism. If democracy is to maintain its essential difference from fascism, it must not compromise on this question of leadership. Leadership, in the sense of the dominance of the community by a single figure, or a minority, is the acknowledged principle of fascism. What, of course, remains in doubt is whether democracy, as a militant organization, can dispense with this principle. What we need, we are told every day, is more and better leadership. But what this demand involves is a closer and closer approximation to fascism. The fascists alone have evolved an efficient form of leadership: efficient leadership is fascism. Opposed to the principle of leadership there is nothing but the principle of equality. Equality is absolute, too; it is a mathematical term, expressing exact quantities. It does not admit of compromise, and whenever I hear a person tampering with this principle in the name of efficiency, or of ability, then I know I am in the presence of a fascist. You may say if you like that equality is not rational—that since people

are not born equal, not equally endowed by nature,[8] that therefore they do not deserve to live equally. But I do not claim that
the principle of equality is a rational doctrine. On the contrary,
it is an irrational dogma, a mystique. It lays down, precisely
because people are born unequal, unequally endowed, they
should in the common interest acknowledge a common
denominator—a standard of citizenship to which all can aspire,
and beyond which none shall venture. I say quite deliberately
that unless we are inspired by that mystical or mythical idea of
social equality, we can not and we do not believe in the
brotherhood of man.

If this dogma is accepted, the practical question remains: how
is it given expression in the organization of a modern community? Bernard Shaw, who saw the necessity for this dogma,
suggested that it can only be given practical expression in equality of incomes. That, of course, is to remain bound to the concept of economic man, which is inevitable in an old-fashioned
Fabian socialist like Shaw. Equality of income might well be the
outward expression of equality of status, but in what other, in
what more fundamental ways, can equality be expressed?

It is curious that we should have to search for an answer to
this question, because in spite of economic and social inequalities we in England have in theory and to some extent in practice
enjoyed what we call 'equality before the law'. Laws might be

---

[8] Matthew Arnold, on the other hand, argues that the love of equality is a
natural expression of the instinct of expansion. 'A thousand arguments may be
discovered in favour of inequality, just as a thousand arguments may be discovered in favour of absolutism. And the one insuperable objection to inequality is the same as the one insuperable objection to absolutism: namely, that
inequality, like absolutism, thwarts a vital instinct, and being thus against
nature, is against our humanization.' But a further remark shows that his
argument is essentially the same as the one used above: 'On the one side, in
fact, inequality harms by pampering; on the other, by vulgarizing and depress-
ing. A system founded on it is against nature, and in the long run breaks
down.'—*Mixed Essays* (1879).

unjust, and the expression of social prejudices rather than of natural equity; nevertheless, for centuries a fair attempt has been made to administer them equally to all men.[9] In fact, you cannot divorce the idea of law from the idea of equity, and that is such a commonplace—such a logical conception, as some might say; such a tradition, as others might say—that we fail to appreciate the fact that it is by no means an inevitable state of affairs. Under fascism we saw a contrary conception of law emerging—one law for the Germans and another law for the races they had subjugated; one law for Aryans and another law for Jews. Eventually Hitler secured the formal abrogation of legal procedure in Germany, and made his personal will superior to the idea of equity. The social hierarchy that we accept almost as a natural order is just as unnatural and illogical as one law for the rich and another for the poor, or as one law for the Germans and another for the conquered Poles. There is no *natural* aristocracy—though there can be an unnaturally cultivated aristocracy, a pedigree stock of human beings no less than a pedigree stock of cattle. The upper classes and the middle classes, the upper middle and the lower middle and the working classes—none of these is a class ordained by nature—they are all expressions of economic inequalities, inequalities that have sometimes lasted for generations. They were continually disturbed, not only by shifting fortunes, but by that displacement which sociologists call the circulation of *élites*, a process which merely expresses the biological fact that luxury and laziness will in the end debilitate the class which enjoys them, and that this class will sink and its place be taken by a class which has led a healthier life. But the circulation of *élites*—an idea very popular with fascist philosophers—is

[9] In so far as they are administered! I am well aware that some people cannot afford 'to go to law', but this injustice is economic and not legal. It should also be clear that I am referring to law as administered in Great Britain, and not to the administration of law in, for example, Spain.

also not a natural phenomenon. At least, it is no more 'natural' than the circulation of water in a boiling kettle: it is an expression of inequalities in social life—inequalities of work and nourishment and recreation. Equalize the temperature of water and it no longer circulates; equalize social conditions, let everybody lead a healthy life, and then you will no longer get a circulation of élites.

And there the fascist philosopher—and some philosophers who call themselves democrats—think they have got you. Ah, they say, no circulation—that means stagnation! And stagnation means decay! War is justified by such people solely on these grounds—that it prevents social stagnation and encourages the emergence of vital stock. A convincing rhetorical attitude can be struck if the circulation metaphor is maintained. But it is merely a figure of speech, a myth. Why all this bubble bubble, toil and trouble? Does not nature offer us alternative metaphors of balance and symmetry, of poise and repose? The best fruit grows on the sheltered wall. The deepest waters are still. To a mind that is still, the whole universe surrenders. How easy it is to find, or invent, convincing metaphors of exactly the opposite tenor. Chinese philosophy is full of them. The universe is full of them. I know that the scientist can present a frightful picture of disintegrating worlds, of exploding suns and cooling planets, of nature red in tooth and claw. But the most fundamental discoveries of science are discoveries of significant design: the periodicity of the elements, the structure of molecules, the universal laws underlying organic forms—these are facts which any reasonable man will make the basis of a positive philosophy.

Lao Tzu, the Great Chinese sage, formulated three rules of political wisdom, which required: (1) abstention from aggressive war and capital punishment, (2) absolute simplicity of living, and (3) refusal to assert active authority. These three rules express the true meaning of social equality. They imply that no man has the right to assert his authority over another man, and that likewise no nation has the right to assert its authority over another nation. If no such right is exercised, by individuals or by nations, then a state of political equality can exist. As for the second rule, which enjoins simple living, that too is not remote from the concept of equality. For the economic complexity of the modern world, involving economic hierarchies and inequalities of income, involving an economic conception of man himself—living man reduced to a commodity, like frozen mutton—this is entirely due to the feverish lust for luxuries. The rule does not deny us plenty: only he that is frugal is truly able to be profuse, says Lao Tzu. Indeed, unless there is plenty, equality can only be maintained by authority; and since we renounce authority, we should ensure plenty. Trotsky once expressed the whole truth in a vivid way: If there is a scarcity of goods in the shops, people will form queues; and if there are queues in the streets, you will have to have police to keep them in order. Law, we might say, is an expression of want.

But it is time I began to draw these observations to some conclusion. I have been questioning the cult of leadership: I assert that it is a denial of the principle of equality. As a counterpart to this cult of leadership we find a state of social irresponsibility, to which I might have devoted more space. But the symptoms of submissiveness, of lethargy and apathy, need no description. I should like to point out, however, that they are not confined to the politically ignorant—I know of no more disastrous example of irresponsibility than the behaviour of the trade unions during the past thirty years. Not only have they repeatedly failed to achieve international unity among the workers of the world: they have been afraid to assume the responsibilities within their grasp at home. I have myself heard one of the leading trade union officials from Transport House declare that the unions had not the necessary managerial ability to control their own industries, and that therefore their policy must be one of compromise and joint control with the employers. That is one instance of what I mean by irresponsibility, and perhaps it deserves a stronger word.

Collective responsibility is the alternative to leadership, and the counterpart of equality. If each individual in the social body is a responsible member of that body there is no need for external control. The body acts as an organic whole, and acts spontaneously. The members of the body-politic are, of course, differentiated according to their function: one is a farmer and another an engineer, one a nurse and another a doctor; and among these members are some whose function is to co-ordinate others. These are the organizers, the administrators and the managers who are essential to a complicated industrial society; but I see no reason why the co-ordinator should be more highly placed or more highly paid than the originator, the creator, the worker. The manager owes his present status and prestige, not to the nature of his work, but to his immediate control of the instruments of production. In any natural society he would be as unobtrusive as a railway signal-man in his box.[10]

I personally believe that life should be immensely simplified—that much of the complexity of modern society is merely the final complication of the sickness we call civilization. But even our elaborate society can be a functional society, and I see no reason why all functions, which are equally necessary to the health of society, should not have social equality. That, at any rate, is the proper meaning of communism, and in this sense communism, the communism of Kropotkin and not that of Marx, is the only alternative to fascism.

Granted all this, my critics will ask: how will you carry on? Somebody must formulate plans, decide on policy, make

---

[10] The pretensions of this group to form a new governing class, so ably analysed by James Burnham in *The Managerial Revolution* (London, 1942), are an inevitable consequence of the cult of leadership in a machine civilization.

decisions on behalf of the whole community. I agree, and would now like to recall the distinction between two kinds of leadership made by Professor Bartlett, which I quoted earlier in this essay; between the kind of leader who *impresses* the group by asserting his authority, and the kind who *expresses* the group by being susceptible to their thoughts, feelings and desires. It is this second kind of leader, and only this kind of leader, who has a place in a community of free people. And who is the leader that expresses the thoughts, feelings and desires of the people—who but the poet and artist? That is the conclusion I have been leading up to. It is not a new idea—it is the conclusion that Plato came to, and that Shelley revived in this country: the idea that it is the man of imagination, the poet and philosopher above all, but equally the man who can present ideas in the visual images of painting and sculpture or through the still more effective medium of drama—the idea that it is this individual whom society should accept as its only leader. Not, of course, at his own valuation. Plato pointed out certain dangers that were to be avoided at all costs. For there are good artists and bad artists, and bad artists are almost more dangerous than bad politicians. Any fruitful analysis of Hitler, for example, must begin with the bad artist rather than the ambitious politician. A free people must therefore be a highly critical people. Such a people does not exist at present, in this or any other country, and it can only be brought into existence by an education and an environment that places first things first—that discounts power and money and competition and all the evil distortions they cause in our social structure and educational ideals.

The evil which is among us, woven into the substance of our life, making us unworthy of equality and incapable of achieving a true democracy, is the evil of assertiveness—the assertiveness of the foreman and the boss, of the captain and the statesman. But it is the assertiveness exercised on the child which is the main evil, for this destroys the unfolding sensibility on which taste and judgement should rest, and plants in its stead the seeds of sadism and masochism. Consider only the assertiveness of the teacher, who significantly claims the title of *master*. He is the first model for the bully, and the early inspiration of the tyrant. It is he who passes on his creed of leadership to the captain of the team and the head of the class: it is he who poisons innocent minds with pride and ambition. How can we expect a libertarian society when our educational system is throughout organized on essentially authoritarian principles? Let us introduce equality into our schools, ask our teachers to be guides and comrades rather than masters and headmasters, and then we shall at least lay the foundations of a community organically free.

'No trace of slavery ought to mix with the studies of a free-born man.' Those words of Plato should be carved above the doors of all our schools and universities, for they express the only condition on which a community of free men can be founded.

5

A CIVILIZATION FROM UNDER

> For the most part we shall be too busy doing the work that lies
> ready to our hands, to let impatience for visibly great progress
> vex us too much; but surely, since we are servants of a Cause,
> hope must be ever with us, and sometimes perhaps it will so
> quicken our vision that it will outrun the slow lapse of time
> and show us the victorious days when millions of those who
> now sit in darkness will be enlightened by an *Art made by the
> people and for the people, a joy to the maker and the user*.
>
> William Morris, *The Beauty of Life*.

Certain general problems connected with the social functions of
the artist tend to be neglected because they are not practical
problems of design in relation to particular objects or particular
industries. In the ordinary course of discussion we simplify the
factors involved. We think of the object to be designed—
something simple and comprehensible enough. We think of the
designer—an individual who has to be brought into relation
with this object. We think of the manufacturer, again as an
individual who has to be persuaded to employ the designer;
and perhaps, if we are considerate enough, we think of the

consumer, again as an individual who has to be persuaded to buy the object designed. It then looks like a simple series of links which have only to be made aware of each other to form an unbroken chain.

But it is not so simple in reality. Just as the economists find that their economic man—the Robinson Crusoe of the textbooks—has little or no correspondence to the mass-man of modern society, so we discover that our designer, our manufacturer and our consumer cannot be considered as isolated units. They are all part of a social complex which cannot be dismantled—which adds up to something more than the sum of its component units.

In the end it turns out that we are not dealing with single or simple units of any kind, but with social groups, vocational groups, national groups, and in general with what we call psychological or ideological factors—habits and fashions which have their roots in tradition, in superstition, in the unconscious levels of the human personality.

It may all be expressed in the old proverb: 'You may take a horse to the trough, but you cannot make him drink.' All our efforts to improve design are useless unless we can persuade the public to adopt them. But that does not express the real necessity. We do not *persuade* the horse to drink; it drinks when it is thirsty. There must arise in the public, therefore, a natural appetite for things of good design. That appetite must exist as a normal state of health.

Now the dogma to which I cling, and for which I could if necessary offer psychological and biological evidence, is that the instinct for what we call good design is an innate possession of every unspoilt human being. It is one of the ironies of history that all the cycles of civilization still leave the savage and the peasant in possession of the surest instinct for the fundamentally right plastic forms. These primitives have not got what we call the brains to design a motor-car or a seaside pavilion, but they never fail to make a good job of a bowl or a basket, a blanket or a boat.

It is logical to conclude, therefore, that it is all a question of education—that if we can bring up our children in such a way that their taste is not corrupted, then this natural instinct for good design will have free play and gradually the whole taste of our time and country will be purified.

A right system of education is, admittedly, going to be one of the principal agents of reform, but the moment you approach this aspect of the problem with any practical intention, you encounter overwhelming difficulties. It is not a question of squeezing in an extra hour for art, or of making handicraft a compulsory instead of an optional subject; it is not even a question of finding teachers with the necessary qualifications. If we are going to solve the problem in this way we shall be faced with the necessity of revising the curricula at every stage of the educational system, because not only must we secure time and opportunity for the *positive* teaching of good design, but we must also make sure that no negative and frustrating tendencies exist elsewhere in the educational system. In other words, it is no good developing the creative and appreciative exercise of the aesthetic impulse in the child if at the same time in some other direction our methods of teaching are inhibiting and deforming this impulse. The whole balance of education, as between intellectual and instinctive activity, must be redressed. Let us frankly face the fact that the joyful expression of rhythm and harmony and colour has nothing whatever to do with logic, reason and memory and the rest of our intellectual fetishes. I am not an anti-intellectualist. I do not say that we had better trust to our instincts in all the affairs of life. But I do say that our educational system is grossly overweighted with intellectual aims; that this rationalization of the child has a stultifying effect on its aesthetic impulse and is directly responsible for the triumph of ugliness in our age.

But the educational difficulties do not end with that immense problem. We may educate the child in school, but outside the school another educational process goes on all the time—the influence of the child's environment. There is no good purpose in developing the creative and appreciative impulses in the child if at the same time we compel it to inhabit ugly schools, to go home through ugly streets and to live in an ugly house surrounded by ugly objects. And so, insensibly we are led to the wider social problem. Education alone will not suffice, because education can only be partial and is perhaps impossible in the chaos of ugliness which the industrial age has created.

It is such considerations as these which may well lead to the conclusion that no good can be done in this sphere unless and until the social system is changed. That seems to be the logical and inevitable conclusion to which we are driven. But at the same time we have to guard against the assumption that we have only to change the social system to secure our aims.

Any large international exhibition is very instructive in this respect. There we see displayed side by side the industrial art of all the countries of the world. It is possible to criticize the display and say that one or another pavilion does not represent the best that a particular nation is capable of. But in any case enough will be seen to establish certain general conclusions of a negative kind. It is quite impossible to find any law of correspondence between the artistic level of the products of the countries represented and their social or political institutions. It is not possible to say that obviously the totalitarian states are making a better job of industrial design than the democratic states, nor apparently to make any correlations between art and politics. The best designs of all, perhaps, come from the small democratic but still capitalist states of Holland, Sweden and Finland. But though we might quarrel in detail about the relative merits of the various national exhibits in such an exhibition, I think we should all agree on the point I am concerned to make: that no particular social system—communism, fascism or capitalism—will necessarily of itself guarantee good design in objects of daily use.

It is simple enough to trace many of the inartistic and decadent qualities in the things we make and use to the prevailing industrial system. The material conditions of poverty which many people support throughout their lives, the lack of leisure and consequential dullness and ignorance—these are the social aspects of the system which prevent any element of quality or discrimination entering into daily life. It is also possible to argue that the very system in its actual mechanism also prevents the emergence of quality—by the division of labour, mass methods of production, economies in material demanded by the universal profit motive. But in fairness it must be pointed out that the system, even under its present economic motivation, can and does produce many objects which have aesthetic qualities, and that we may fail to perceive these qualities because of our anti-industrial prejudices. I refer to the aeroplanes and motor-cars and other typical products of the modern industrial system which are by no means devoid of those elements of beauty which we find in classical art. I do not wish to insist on this aspect of the question, but it should serve to warn us that there is no necessary connection between the economic and even the ethical characteristics of an industrial system and the aesthetic merits of the products of that system.

Let us turn for a moment to the positive evidence offered by the case of Russia. In one vast industrial area, amounting to one-sixth of the world, the old economic system has been destroyed by revolution and a new economic system has been established which gradually eliminated the profit motive and gave the workers of Russia indirect control of the processes of production. The technical features of capitalist production remain, and have even been intensified. Division of labour and mass production remain. There is still little leisure, and though there is no longer acute poverty, there is no great abundance. It is still an economy of scarcity, and it is still a money economy. Workers are paid wages according to the kind and amount of work they do, and the more they produce the more they are paid.

It is not necessary for me to go into all the details of the Soviet system; the very act of presenting them might arouse controversy. The most general and most significant feature of the whole Soviet economy, distinguishing it from ours and from every other system in the world, is that it is centrally controlled for the total benefit of the people. This centralization means not only that the kind and quantity of goods are planned on a national scale, but also that there is every possibility of controlling the quality. And great efforts are made to this end. Artists and designers are organized in co-operatives, and their services are placed at the disposal of the soviets and factories. We all know what a great part museums and exhibitions play in the social life of the country, and even more direct encouragement is given to artists. 'Annually [to quote one authority[1]] the Council of People's Commissars now offers monetary awards to men and women who have attained distinction in the arts. In 1941 these awards embraced music, painting, sculpture, architecture, theatre, opera, dramatic writing, ballet, motion pictures, fiction, poetry, literary criticism. In each division three to five artists receive a first award of 100,000 roubles each, and from three to ten a second award of half that sum.' Such a deliberate promotion of culture continues to the present day.

From all this it would seem that Russia must be an earthly paradise for the artist, and undoubtedly the artist is treated with more respect in Russia than anywhere else in the world. Let me quote one more witness—a well-known American sculptress, Emma Lu Davis:

'In the Spring of 1935 I went to Russia. I wanted to see how

[1] Maurice Hindus, *Russia Fights On* (London, 1942), p. 127.

the artists were organized over there, how they were utilized in the scheme of life, and how socialized patronage affected the arts. I found that from an economic-social standpoint the Soviet artist enjoys the happiest situation in the world; as a trade union member he enjoys protection and social security, he never lacks employment, and building and decorative projects are broad enough to include all varieties of work—*except good work*. This, I believe, was in no way the fault of socialism. Soviet artists are not regimented any more than artists in other countries, but it happens that the pressure of popular taste is toward bad and tawdry styles in painting and sculpture. Russia has not a broad or intelligent popular base of appreciation of real beautiful projects. The Russian tradition of real folk painting disappeared four or five hundred years ago with the last of the fine ikons. Since then there has been nothing but a second-rate tradition of academic paint and clay pushing.'[2]

The significant fact which emerges from all the evidence we can collect about the situation of the artist in Russia is that in spite of a fundamental change in the economic system, and in spite of all this direct encouragement of the arts by those in authority, there has not been anything in the nature of an artistic renaissance. In spite of state-supported artists' co-operatives, in spite of large monetary awards and official honours, in spite of a socialized and centrally planned economy, Russia does not turn out for the admiration of the world pots which are better than the pots we make in Staffordshire, glassware which is better than the glassware of Sweden, furniture which is better than the furniture of Finland, films which are better than the films of America, paintings and sculpture which are better than the paintings and sculpture of France or Italy. Its theatre, its opera and its ballet may be as good or better than anything of their·

---

[2] *Americans,* 1942 (New York: Museum of Modern Art), p. 44.

kind in Europe, but these are arts that are traditionally good in Russia, and that have no direct relation to the economic system.

This is a very significant and even a very disturbing fact, and it should be examined dispassionately, without the least trace of political bias. It is a scientific problem. A nation has taken certain measures to produce certain results. In one respect the experiment failed. We are about to make the same experiment. Let us take care not to make the same mistake.

I believe the mistake is fundamentally this: You cannot impose a culture from the top—it must come from under. It grows out of the soil, out of the people, out of their daily life and work. It is a spontaneous expression of their joy in life, of their joy in work, and if this joy does not exist, the culture will not exist. Joy is a spiritual quality, an impalpable quality; that too cannot be forced. It must be an inevitable state of mind, born of the elementary processes of life, a by-product of natural human growth. Obviously there are material conditions which favour its emergence. A people cannot be joyful if it is hungry or poverty-stricken, if it is stricken by war or oppression. Unfortunately the Russian people have been hungry and poor, threatened by war and oppressed. We cannot, therefore, sit in academic judgement on the quality of their culture. But I think it is evident enough that the worst kind of oppression came from within. The first authority I quoted just now, an observer who has written many sympathetic books about the Soviet régime, goes on to say that these men and women who compete for the awards offered to the artists, and others like them, 'have had to speak the political language, the political thought of the Kremlin, which, with no concession to difference of opinion or will, has, in its own way, been ruthlessly driving the nation everywhere, to its own formula of living, its own steely resolve to convert the country as rapidly as possible into a far-flung military fortress'.

Today no one conscious of the efficiency of that far-flung military fortress, and of all that it meant to our own security and eventual survival in the Second World War, has any right to question that ruthless aim, in spite of all it has entailed in cultural shortcomings. We have not the right, and I hope not the impudence, to criticize Russia in this respect because our own priorities have been the same. We must patiently observe the sociological processes that are taking place under our eyes. If we do that in the spirit of science and realism, then I do not think we can avoid the conclusion that this centralized control of the arts and of all modes of artistic expression has defeated its own end in Russia. The arts, we may conclude—and not only from this vast modern experiment, but from the vaster experiment of human evolution—can only thrive in an atmosphere of liberty. Artists may be prosperous under a tyranny, and most dictators, conscious of the judgement of history, try to weave a cloak of culture to hide their misdeeds. But the judgement of history is absolute, and when tyrants and artists have passed away, the art remains, to be tried by laws which are neither economic nor utilitarian, but solely aesthetic.

I suggest that certain broad conclusions emerge from all these confusing issues. I think we can state that a vital culture requires in the first place an economic system that guarantees a certain measure of security to a class, and preferably to a whole people. I do not want to confuse security with wealth, or even with comfort: some of the finest art in the world has been produced by peasants, and even by the people we call savages. In the second place, I think we may conclude that a vital culture requires spiritual liberty—freedom to express individual feelings and aspirations without fear of condemnation. Security and freedom—these are, as it were, the external conditions for the emergence of a great culture. But external conditions are not enough, and no social system, regimentary or liberal, totalitarian or democratic, will achieve a native style of art unless that style has a wide basis in the natural taste of the people at large. This is the essential internal condition, and though it has its outward aspect, which we might describe as vitality, it is really a spiritual energy that cannot be consciously cultivated by the individual. It springs from social integration, from the satisfaction of common needs, from mutual aid and from unity of aspiration.

I say we cannot cultivate such spiritual energy self-consciously as individuals, and by this I mean that it cannot be inspired by preaching or spread by propaganda. But naturally we can and must provide the conditions suitable to its emergence, and these conditions are, not only the security and freedom essential to the artist as an individual, but also a mode of upbringing or system of education that is social rather than individual in its methods and ideals. This is a subject which I have dealt with in a separate book,[3] but I must give a clue to my meaning. The word 'education' implies many things, but in our modern practice it is always a process of individuation, of developing individual or separate qualities—what schoolmasters and politicians call 'character'—qualities which distinguish the individual from his group or environment. The development of such qualities in the individual is very necessary, essential to the variety of our democratic way of life. But in itself this kind of education is socially disintegrating, and it should be accompanied by some process which corrects the tendency towards disintegration, and brings the individual back into the social unit. In primitive societies— societies which are nearly always remarkable for the cohesion of their culture and the vitality of their way of life—there exists such a process. Instead of 'education' we find certain rites of 'initiation'—a drawing of the individual into society, to merge him with the group. We use the same word in connection with religious communities—and always with the implication of a leading 'in', and not a drawing 'out'. Education should be balanced by initiation—a drawing of the individual into the community, making him conscious of its collective life, its collective

[3] *Education Through Art*. New edition, London (Faber & Faber), 1958.

ideals and aspirations. We vaguely realize this truth in our attempt to create a youth movement. But I mean something much more intimate and far-reaching than anything implied in such social patchwork. I mean a conception of education that is socialized from the kindergarten up, in which every classroom is a busy little workshop, every schoolboy a novice seeking initiation into the mysteries of art and science, every lesson a group activity, binding and inspiring the individual, creating that collective consciousness which is the spiritual energy of a people and the only source of its art and culture.

Now if that is true—if this interpretation of the obvious facts is admitted—then it must make a difference to our policy. It is only too easy—I confess it has often been my own state of mind—to give up the direct struggle for an immediate object in the hope or expectation that a social revolution of some sort will change everything for the better, including in its general sweep the aim for which we have been so vainly struggling. But that is disproved by the evidence of recent years. In no single case can it be said that a social or economic revolution has brought about a higher standard of public taste. If anything, the evidence shows that unless accompanied by an intelligent system of education, an increase in the social and economic well-being of any group of people only leads to an expansion of vulgarity and bad taste.

It follows that we must strive now and always for our immediate objectives. Our struggle is on the artistic or aesthetic plane, and to secure our ends, to establish our purely aesthetic ideals, we must be prepared to think outside the categories of the existing political systems. In particular, we must abandon the idea that all our problems can be solved by 'the state'. I do not question the power of the state: it is said that the Mother of Parliaments can do all things, even unto changing the sex of her citizens. But that is not the point. In so far as it is a question of preserving life and property, of securing decency and cleanliness, the state now acts with an almost excessive thoroughness.

But it almost completely ignores the equally important questions of what I will call public appearances—the colour and shape and visual agreeableness of what everybody has to see and use every day of their lives. It is difficult to understand why the state, which prevents a man from getting drunk or committing a felony, should not only allow but even encourage this same man to foul the public vision with an ugly house or a hideous piece of furniture. It can only be because the state as such is an expression of purely economic values. In any less materialistic standard of values the sin of ugliness would rank a good deal higher than the sin of covetousness.

We need a reform of public taste—a vast cultural movement comparable to the religious Reformation of the sixteenth century. But a reformation is a violent process; it doesn't just happen. It means breaking down old habits, making new associations, adapting ourselves to new conditions. It is a difficult and uncomfortable experience for the majority of people, and the majority of people are just not going to bother to reform themselves if it involves conscious effort. We must not forget that the Englishman's home is his castle, and that he quite instinctively, and quite rightly, resents the interference of people who propose to invade his private domain, and not merely invade it, but pass rude remarks about what they find there—the china and the curtains, the carpets and the chairs, even the ornaments on the mantelpiece. And that is the attitude not only of the man in the street, but also of the manufacturers of such carpets and chairs and ornaments. Such people resent the activities of the reformer still more bitterly—to them we are just obnoxious interlopers trying to tell them how to run their business.

There is, of course, a technique for dealing with the manufacturer. We can point out to him—indeed we can prove to him—that what we call good design is a commercial asset, and that in a world of shrinking markets, where the manufacturer can depend less and less on the exploitation of new consumers, the appearance and quality of his goods is going to be the determining factor. But our obligations do not end with the conversion of the manufacturer, much as that is to be desired. We must still work on the imponderables—public taste, public education, the general level of culture in the masses.

I have said that you cannot impose a culture from the top—it must be a by-product of the natural productive activity of the people. But this does not mean that we must just sit back and wait for the miracle to happen. Regeneration will begin at the bottom, in the family, in the school, in the workshop and in the parish and the borough. Action will be regional rather than national, but we might make a beginning with those institutions which are already subject to regional and communal control. Already a vast amount of production and distribution is carried out by public or semi-public bodies which might take the lead in those 'rites of initiation' that give the individual a social morality and a pride in public appearances. When we consider that it is our ambition not only to improve the design of pots and pans, of furniture and textiles, but also of public buildings like town halls and railway stations, council houses and government offices, of roads and all they carry in the way of signposts and lighting systems; when we consider, moreover, that a democratic organization like the Co-operative Movement is one of the worst offenders in the field of design—then we shall begin to see why we must create a public conscience in this matter. We must create a public standard of taste (decent design) comparable to the public standard of behaviour (decent conduct—which does exist though it is not always observed). And design in something more tangible than conduct.

Bernard Shaw once said with reference to the proposed national theatre: 'It is a simple historical fact that cultural institutions have to be imposed on the masses by rulers or private patrons enlightened enough to know that such institutions are neither luxuries nor mere amusements but necessities of civilized life.' I don't agree with this dictum: I believe that cultural institutions 'imposed on' the masses are so much dead weight—to hell with such culture! But this does not mean that the taste of a people should not find spontaneous expression in national institutions, and I would like to see, not only a National Gallery and a National Theatre, but also a National Cinema, a National Ballet, and a national institution for the exhibition of the beautiful things created by a people's industry. We need not call it a Museum—that conveys the notion of a place where the past is preserved. We want a place where the future is forecast. Let us call it, therefore, the House of Good Design, and let it be worthy of the power and potentialities of our industries; let there be at least one cathedral to commemorate the achievements of the Machine Age.

I realize that I have not yet answered the simple and devastating question: to what end? Why should we take this trouble and expend this energy for the sake of something so intangible as beauty? There is the economic argument already used, but the economist might turn on us and say: let us rather have a League of Industrial Peace to eliminate all competitive factors, among them design. After all, from a strictly economic point of view, there is no need to make things beautiful so long as they function satisfactorily. No; in the end we must abandon the economic arguments. We must use it for strategic purposes, but finally we shall have to confess that beauty is its own end: that we are fighting for better design as part of a better world. In the end our argument is not economic, nor practical, nor even ethical; it is simply biological. We may have the conviction—certainly I have—that there is a final correspondence between what is efficient and what is beautiful and what is true: a conviction that art is a human contribution to the universal design. But our front is definite, our scope is strict: we concentrate on one aspect of the necessary revolution, while admitting that this necessary revolution is necessarily total. We realize that the vulgarity of which we complain runs through the whole fabric of our civilization. We have no feeling for beauty because we have no respect for truth and goodness. Eric Gill used to say that if we got our moral and religious values right, the rest would follow: beauty would look after herself. With qualifications which involve a whole theory of aesthetics and a whole philosophy of life, I would agree. But at the conclusion of an essay which is already long enough I can only make these bleak affirmations:

> Beauty is a quality in things made—'the radiance of things made as they ought to be made' (Gill).
>
> Beauty is therefore something that appeals directly to the senses.
>
> An epoch of art becomes possible only when workmen are not concerned to make things beautifully, are not *told* to make things beautifully, but do so just because they don't know any worse.
>
> A great civilization or culture can only arise on the basis of a natural instinct to make things as they ought to be made.

And that is why I call it a civilization 'from under'.

6

THE SYMPTOMS OF DECADENCE

I implore you to tell me how a people that has so many philosophers can have so little taste. . . .

Voltaire in a letter to the Cardinal de Bernis

You seem to be surprised that philosophy, enlightening the mind and rectifying ideas, should have so little influence on the taste of a nation. You are quite right: and yet you will have observed that manners have even more empire over taste than have the sciences. It seems to me that in the matter of art and of literature, the progress of taste is more dependent on the spirit of society than on the philosophic spirit.

The Cardinal de Bernis in a letter to Voltaire. Cited by Delacroix, *Journal*, April 9, 1858.

The symptoms of decadence as they reveal themselves in the art of a country are indifference, vanity and servitude. Indifference is the absence of appreciation: it is the general attitude towards the arts in an industrial age. It is true that we still have a few patrons who carry on a bygone system, but they are neither numerous enough nor influential enough to affect the general body of art. It is significant, too, that they confine themselves to the arts of painting and music, whose products can be used for their personal profit—for the decoration of their houses or the amusement of their friends. I know of no modern patrons of poetry, or of literature of any kind. A poet might sell his autograph for sixpence at a charity bazaar, but it would be a poor sort of bazaar that could not procure the far more valuable services of a racing motorist, a county cricketer or a film star.

Indifference is endemic. It is a disease which has spread through our whole civilization, and which is a symptom of a lowered vitality. The sensibilities are dulled and the average human being no longer cares to feel the keen edge of life, to have freshness in vision or zest and savour in the senses. He prefers to face life in the armour of boredom and cynicism, fending off despair with the brazen shield of dissipation. If he is rich he can command amusements that soothe his exacerbated nerves without engaging his mind or intriguing his imagination; if he is poor he will plunge into the cheap make-believe world of Hollywood where he can enjoy vicariously the glittering life of the rich; or he will gamble his ill-spared shillings on the football pools in the expectation of one day being able to indulge in his own hectic spending. But rich or poor, it is the same fever to escape from reality—above all, from art, which is the mirror in which the reality of life is accentuated.

There is one exception to this rule: those people who think they can subdue the artist and use his works for their own profit. The time has gone by in which any credit is to be obtained by the direct patronage of art; no one, for the sake of a dedication, would pay a poet to write an epic. But certain kinds of art can be brought within the orbit of the commercial system—that is to say, they can be given an artificial scarcity value and put on the market. This applies above all to movable objects like paintings. But the process by which a painting becomes a market commodity is not a simple one. The demand must be created and the supply must be restricted. I do not want to suggest that the demand can be created irrespective of merit; but granted the merit, it must be exploited, and it can only be exploited by snobbish means. A painter might paint fifty pictures a year and make quite a good living by selling them at £20 apiece to a wide anonymous public; but in that way he would never become famous in his lifetime. By devious ways it has to be suggested that a few select people should pay £1000 for the rare privilege of possessing one of Mr. Xs' canvases. And such is the cunning and efficiency of the art trade that this can be done. But then consider the position of this lucky and perhaps deserving artist. His pictures pass from his studio to the dealer's rack; from this emporium they are doled out to the public at a rate which will not flood the market. They are priced as high as the audacious dealer dares, and bought by someone rich enough to pay this exorbitant sum. A situation has been created in which the work of art is bought, not for its intrinsic value as a work of art, but simply because it is a commercial rarity the possession of which will reflect credit on the owner.

In such a situation there is no organic relation between the artist and the public; there is no real contact, no give and take of expression and appreciation. The artist is working in a closed circuit, and need never break it.

The danger in this situation is not that the artist makes a good living and is able to live a life of luxury. Good artists in the past, such as Rubens, have lived like princes and no harm has come to their art. But Rubens lived in direct contact with his public; he dealt, as it were, across his own counter. The modern artist is as remote as the mines of Anaconda or Rio Tinto, and subject to the same quotations and speculations. And very much the same motives govern both markets. The prices of pictures are not quoted in the Stock Exchange lists, but they have their fluctuations on Vanity Fair. So have most of the commodities of the art market. The publisher must exploit vanity for his books, the impresario for his music and the producer for his plays. The only alternative is to substitute entertainment for art. The public will pay for entertainment; the private person for the privilege of possessing something unique.

Vanity in the patron of art leads to servitude in the artist. A servile mind is a mind that has committed moral suicide. Art is independence—independence of vision, directness of expression, spiritual detachment. A good deal of nonsense has been written about the anonymous artists of the Middle Ages. If we do not know the names of the architects of our cathedrals or of the sculptors and painters who decorated them, it is simply because the artists of the period did not have the benefit of a modern publicity service; the records have perished: the art remains, universal and therefore impersonal in its appeal, but none the less the creation of individual minds. If Adam Lock, the thirteenth-century architect of Wells Cathedral, or William Wynford, the fourteenth-century architect of Winchester, are not so well known as Wren or Nash, it is not that they were inferior as architects, or in any sense less individual. We can affirm it as a simple fact that from the earliest appearance of art in prehistoric times until the present day, art has been the creation of individual minds, reacting freely to their environment, expressing and interpreting the common will, but deriving the essence and the vitality of their works from the make and manner of their own personalities.

It is because art is such an individual act of creation that it demands freedom for its perfection—freedom of mind and freedom of person. It is often objected to this point of view that some of the greatest works of art were produced in times of stress—that the Divine Comedy was written by a political exile, and Don Quixote in a jail. But if we look more closely into these cases, we find that Dante approximates to a distinguished political exile of today spending his time as a guest in various country-houses—not bad conditions for poetic activity; and as for Cervantes, prison was a peaceful and carefree interval in a life of poverty and persecution.

The truth is rather that there is scarcely a great artist in the history of modern civilization whose work would not have been incomparably greater if he could have lived in spiritual freedom and economic security. There exists a fragment of a letter from Leonardo da Vinci to his patron, Ludovic Sforza. 'I regret very much,' he wrote, 'that the fact of my having to gain my living should have prevented me from continuing the work which your Highness has intrusted to me: but I hope that within a short time I shall have earned so much as to be able with a tranquil mind to satisfy your Excellency, to whom I commend myself. If your Excellency thought that I had money, you were deceived, for I have had six mouths to feed for thirty-six months, and I have had fifty ducats.' This man had perhaps the greatest intellect that the human race has ever produced: he was hindered and reduced to impotency for the want of a few ducats.

The economic servitude of the artist is one cause of the death of art, and there is no age which can escape the shame of keeping its artists in poverty. But poverty is nevertheless an experience from which the artist can derive some benefit, such as a sympathetic understanding of the sufferings of humanity and a knowledge of the behaviour of men in adversity. A certain apprenticeship in humility is perhaps essential to the development of the artist. But there is no sanction at all for that other form of servitude which springs from intolerance. It is understandable that politicans should resent the power of effective expression which is in the hands of the artist, and that they should want to control this power in the interests of a system of government or a policy. It is understandable that a church should want to use this power to propagate its dogmas. Art is not inconsistent with such propaganda, so long as the artist is consenting, or believing, or sympathizing. But that the further step should be taken, and that art should be controlled by politicians in its own supposed interests, is simply catastrophic. Art may suffer determination of aim, and still survive in however debased a form; but that the artist should submit to a dictation of method is inconceivable. In the very act of submission he ceases to be an artist. To declare that the art of a country should be of a particular style—it is always a style from the past—or of a particular content—heroic, realist, moral or eugenic: such action immediately inhibits the artist, and art comes to a sudden end. It is for this reason, and this reason alone, that no considerable works of art have emerged from Russia since about 1924.

It is not that art is incompatible with revolution—far from it. Nor do I suggest that art has no specific part to play in a revolutionary struggle. I am not defending art for art's sake; I am not arguing that art should remain 'pure'—such art is generally the art of the reactionary dilettanti. Art as I have defined it is so intimately linked to the vital forces of life that it carries society towards ever new manifestations of that life. Art, in its full and free subjective action, is the one essentially revolutionary force with which man is endowed. Art is revolution, and art can best serve revolution by remaining true to itself.

Art's wider significance is biological. It is no idle play of surplus energies, no mere lustre on the hard surface of reality, as materialists have tended to argue. It springs from the centre of life. It is the finest tone of our vitality, the reflexion of harmonious form, the very echo of the organic rhythm of the universe. A nation without art may achieve external order; it may accumulate wealth and exercise power. But if it is without aesthetic sensibility, these things will perish as if from their own weight, their lack of balance and proportion. Perhaps no civilization is destined to survive many centuries, but when a civilization is stricken, we shall then notice, along with a declining birth-rate and an increasing debt, first the censure of originality in art and then art's complete subservience and defeat. The decline and fall of a civilization naturally involve the decline and fall of its art; but it is a mistake to assume that art perishes simply because its social foundations are withdrawn. The foundations are the art, and they perish from a rot that has invaded the whole structure. Psychologists say that our minds contain two contrary impulses—the will to live and the will to die; and that the curve of life is the result of the contest between them. So with a civilization. It has a will to live and a will to die; and the highest expression of its will to live is a free and original art.

7

THE COLLECTIVE PATRON

One of the reasons why I am out of employment now, why I
have been out of employment for years, is simply that I have
other ideas than the gentlemen who give the places to men
who think as they do.

Vincent van Gogh, Letter to his Brother Theo,
July 1880.

I have suggested, on an earlier page, that the artist should be
abolished: art is not a separate 'profession', but a quality inherent in all work well done. I have also implied that in a healthy
society the citizens are not too conscious of their 'culture': they
create works of art automatically, instinctively. At the same time
I admitted that there were certain 'glittering pinnacles' which
pierce through the routine of daily activity, to achieve a timeless
universality.

In order that these sun-capped peaks shall emerge in the
course of a nation's evolution, it is necessary that there should be
a general diffusion of sensibility, that people should possess
natural 'taste'. Taste is formed by a continuous assessment of

quality such as all craftsmen instinctively direct towards each other's work. In society as a whole a critical attitude of this kind produces a progressive awareness of the formal beauty of human artifacts, and this is the true meaning of 'taste'.

If I am asked whether this is a necessary or a healthy activity, I hesitate to be positive. Self-consciousness in art is the beginning of sophistication, and if it means a loss of social consciousness in the individual, a sense of separateness, I am sure it is the beginning of the end, the first symptom of social decadence. But criticism can be group criticism: it can be the social awareness of social relevance, and in that sense it is a necessary function. It is the sense of quality, the recognition of achievement. It is the collective appreciation and promotion of art.

In a vital community, art is promoted in three ways: socially by appreciation, economically by patronage, and essentially by liberty. These are the three necessities upon which the life of art depends: appreciation, patronage and liberty.

We need not dwell on the need for appreciation. There have been artists who had lived and worked without immediate appreciation, but they have been inspired by conviction—by a fanatical faith in the eventual recognition of their genius. Artists like Van Gogh have so much confidence in themselves that they are content to work for a posterity they will never see. But such individuals are very rare. Even the most neglected artists usually have a small circle of devoted admirers, and even two or three spirits of rare perception are sufficient to confirm an artist in his activity. Indeed, there is every reason to distrust more than a moderate success in one's own time: every great artist being under the necessity, as Wordsworth said, of creating the public taste by which he is appreciated—a process that takes time. The essential thing is for the artist to have the sense of an audience: to feel that his voice is not echoing in an empty room, with no response. In every great artist's development there is an imperceptible process of give and take, of appeal and response, of trial and experiment—and he cannot experiment on a dead and unresponsive body.

The second necessity for the life of art is *patronage*: a word which I use deliberately. There are two ways in which an artist can live: by selling his art to the public, or by receiving an income not dependent on his artistic activity. In spite of everything that has been said to the contrary, I am convinced that independence is the only proper basis for any kind of creative activity. I do not wish to revive the private patronage which became current in this country during the seventeenth century and persisted until more recent times: that had its obvious abuses, and was in fact a form of servile dependence, however enlightened the patron might be. But, unsatisfactory as such personal bonds might be, the commercialization of art which followed was much more disastrous, and I can think of no artist—certainly not artists like Scott or Balzac or Dickens—who would not have been better artists if they had been relieved of insistent financial pressure. It is a fact of no small significance that a great majority of the painters, poets and composers who have risen to fame since the disappearance of the patronage system have been men with independent incomes derived from inherited estates. Or, like Wordsworth, they have been in possession of official sinecures during a considerable part of their lives.

It is instructive to observe how the problem of the artist's income has been dealt with in a new society like the socialist republic of Russia. The evidence published by various interested parties is conflicting, but briefly we may say that the arts are divorced from the industries (a sculptor, for example, belonging to an artist's 'collective' or union, and not to the same union as a stonemason) and organized on parallel lines. There exist co-operative unions for all the various branches of art, with head offices in Moscow and branches all over the U.S.S.R. Any artist, on producing evidence of his talent and of his serious intentions, may join the appropriate co-operative. When he has been properly admitted, he then signs a contract of a year's duration. In this contract the artist binds himself to hand over to the co-operative his year's work, and the co-operative in return undertakes to pay him a monthly sum—a minimum of 500 roubles for unknown artists, rising to 2000 roubles or more for artists of established reputation.

The co-operatives do not seem to have any difficulty in disposing of the works supplied by the artists: 'fine' art, in that vast republic of 180 million souls, is a scarcity commodity. The difficulty is the artist. He may not produce the quantity of work specified in the contract. For a time the co-operative may allow him to continue in its debt, but finally there is a crisis and the artist is expelled. On the other hand, if the artist produces more than he promised, and the co-operative disposes of it all, he is entitled to his share of the surplus.

This system is admittedly far in advance of anything existing in capitalist countries, but from the point of view of the artist it has two serious defects. It puts a premium on productivity or facility, and it allows the co-operative, and the Central Art Committee which controls all the co-operatives, to dictate the kind of art that should or must be produced. The first objection might not seem very grave to the public at large, whose work is necessarily of a routine character. And admittedly there are many artists—perhaps the great majority—who can turn out their paintings by the square foot and their books by the page with the regularity of a shoemaker or a riveter. But the exceptional artist—and it is the exceptions that we are considering—can conform to no such measured pace. He is dependent on endless experimentation, on a slow process of gestation, and on fitful inspiration. He works by intuition and not by rule of thumb; he may need five years to produce a single masterpiece; short periods of creative activity are followed by long periods of equally creative inactivity. Art divorced from industry is no longer an industry, and cannot be governed by the principles of industrial organization.

But serious as this defect is, it is not so harmful as the discipline and censorship which such a form of organization permits and even implies. The co-operatives are in effect a part of the state machine, and a close control of them is exercised by the Central Art Committee, which is the equivalent of a Ministry of Fine Art working under the direction of the central government. Now, art is too closely related to education and propaganda to be neglected by a totalitarian régime, and the control of art in Russia has in consequence become increasingly strict, with fatal results. I am not referring to anything that might be excused as political censorship. Art has been condemned and artists imprisoned or exiled for purely stylistic reasons. There are Russian artists in Europe and America who have had to leave their country, not because they were politically suspect, but merely because they would not paint in a naturalistic style. There are architects who have been exiled because they refused to build in the neo-classic style of their grandfathers. Poets and composers are in disgrace because their verses do not rhyme or their tunes are not melodic. And for every one of these artists who are known to us we may be sure there are many who are mute because they refuse to submit to the indignity of all such restrictions made in the interests of vulgarity or dogmatism.

Patronage of some kind is essential, but it is only tolerable when accompanied by liberty. Patronage need not imply servitude. True patronage is a tribute to the genius of the artist and a recognition of the fact that the quality we call art cannot be assessed in economic terms. I call it a tribute, but this does not imply that it should be a charity. The demand for art, when organized, will be quite capable of supporting the artist. The Russian system, in its broad outlines, is essentially the right system for a society committed to industrialization. Free it from bureaucratic regimentation, free it from political intolerance, and then the artist's collective could ensure, not only a basic livelihood for all its members, but liberty to work at an individual pace and in an individual manner.

Art, in its collective aspect, would become the patron of individual artists. The evil of the old system of patronage sprang from the individualism of the patron. It was the patron's vanity, his desire to use the artist for his own glorification, or for the defence of his interests, that demoralized the artist. No artist ever suffered from the gift of a sinecure or the grant of a pension. But art itself was in danger because its economic basis was dependent on the will of an individual who was not himself an artist, and who had not necessarily any understanding of art.

An artist's collective has an historical analogy in the craft guilds of the Middle Ages, but admittedly, in the modern sense and under modern conditions, it is an untried experiment. But I see no alternative which would give the artist economic independence and liberty of action. The true solution of this problem, as I have insisted again and again in my writings, is the reintegration of art and work, so that art becomes simply the qualitative aspect of all that is made and done and said in a community. Apart from this, there is only the possibility that the artist of the future should earn his living in some quite different vocation and practise his art in his hours of leisure. That is, of course, the condition under which many artists work today. But what sort of conception of art have we if we imagine that it can be produced by tired workers at weekends? Art in any worthy sense is not only arduous, but demands a continuous application of the faculties; it requires the full disposition of the whole man, if not in actual labour, then in observation, contemplation and passive awareness. Art is a full-time job.

The reintegration of art and work, as I have defined it elsewhere in this book, would absorb most of our 'professional' artists: the architect, the sculptor, the painter, the composer, each has a natural niche in the industrial hierarchy. Only the poet is excluded—the poet in the widest sense, the seer or visionary in any medium of expression. The 'divine literatus' is a social outcast. He is the product of his 'contrary experience'.

If the liberty of the artist could be guaranteed by his guild, then he would, of course, have corresponding duties, a responsibility not only to his guild, but also to the community as a whole. But such duties are too intangible to be defined, or can be defined with simplicity and truth as the duty to be a good artist. It is sometimes said that the artist is under an obligation to make himself understood. But understood by whom? By 'the man in the street'? Obviously not, otherwise we should have to condemn the greater part of our poetry and music. By a select few? Possibly, but only if that few remain hidden and anonymous; for a coherent few becomes a sect or clique, and their demands revive all the abuses of the old system of patronage. The artist is really responsible to a body more universal and remote: to humanity in its widest consciousness and finest power of perception. There are many artists of talent, but greatness lies precisely in this power to realize and even to forecast the imaginative needs of mankind.

8

THE SECRET OF SUCCESS

In this essay I propose to discuss the social laws and customs that determine the success of artists. We cannot begin with the assumption that it is simply a question of genius or talent, for we know that many artists who are later recognized as great artists had no success in their lifetime, and that many of those who enjoyed success in their lifetime are later forgotten. It is also obvious that the success of an artist in his lifetime is sometimes based on qualities different from those for which he is admired by a later age. There is therefore a very complex interrelationship of several factors, among which it may not be easy to trace the operation of any definite laws—chance may indeed play a great part in a field where so many of the factors are subjective or emotional.

Genius is difficult to define, and we should perhaps limit ourselves to a consideration of the more modest endowment which we call *talent*. The man of genius is always an 'outsider'—what genius does, as Goethe said, is done unconsciously, and the success or the unsuccess that attends the work of genius is not the result of the operation of any social laws. A genius is like a comet which for a brief moment flashes across the night sky and disturbs the normal pattern of stars; or, to speak less metaphorically, genius is a biological 'sport' and not representative of the species artist.

We cannot exclude unconscious factors from our discussion, as I shall indicate later; but for the moment I would like to consider the normal maturation of a talent, in painting for example, and ask what qualities in the artist and what conditions in society make for success. With qualities so various and conditions so inconstant, any generalization will be difficult.

Let us begin with the artist. We shall assume an initial endowment, an innate sensibility which at the approach of adulthood manifests itself in the desire to be an artist. Here begins the first hazard—the choice of a profession. It is by no means certain that the individual in question, on the basis of a diffused aesthetic sensibility, will hit upon the right craft. Paul Klee hesitated between painting and music, and we are glad that he chose painting. But to take a painter of another age, Benjamin Robert Haydon (1786–1846)—this artist, in the belief that he was born to be a great historical painter, expended passionate energy, and for a time was able to convince his contemporaries (or some of them) that he was a great genius; but in the end he failed miserably and committed suicide. He left behind a *Journal* which is one of the most interesting documents in the literature of art, brilliantly written, and there can be little doubt that if Haydon had chosen to be a writer instead of a painter, he might have ranked with Scott or Balzac.

Let us assume that the potential artist does not make a mistake of this kind—that he makes the right choice of craft. The development of his talent will then depend on several factors, the first and most obvious being his physical and mental health. His sensibility is already a reflection of his constitution, and this in its turn is conditioned by hereditary factors and by his early upbringing (again we are directed to the unconscious, for his talent may depend on such factors as the successful sublimation of aggressive instincts, the resolution of the Oedipal situation, integration of the personality, etc.). The will to be an artist emerges from tremendous inner conflicts of this kind, and it is only when all these have been resolved (and it is a problem which involves the individual's relationship to society as a whole as well as to his immediate family environment), only then can he face the still considerable hazards of an artistic career.

The first of such hazards is education—by which I mean education outside the upbringing he receives in his family, public education. This is perhaps the greatest hazard of all, because there is no doubt that most systems of education might have been designed deliberately to stultify the aesthetic sensibility of a child. With rare exceptions public education throughout the world today concentrates on the inculcation of intellectual knowledge, for which it requires the development of such faculties as memory, analysis, enumeration, classification and generalization. These are faculties that may either deaden or depress the aesthetic sensibility, which needs for its development concreteness, sensational acuteness, emotional spontaneity, attention, contemplation, wholeness of vision or apprehension, and generally what Keats called 'negative capability'.

The conflict between the intellectual and the aesthetic approach to education was first clearly realized by Schiller and his *Aesthetische Briefe* remain the clearest statement of this inescapable dilemma, a dilemma which is not likely to be resolved by our rationalistic civilization. My own view, which I have presented in several books, is that the psychic imbalance of the prevailing systems of education is directly responsible for the moral delinquency of our populations and their inevitable drift to annihilating wars, but that is a wider aspect of the problem. For the moment I am concerned with the education of the artist, and we may see that the only great artists in our civilization are those who have managed, either by chance or by deliberate effort, to avoid the deleterious effects of conventional education. The public image of the artist is of precisely such a person—the Bohemian, the Outsider—a man who behaves and even dresses differently from 'the man in the street'. In a rationalistic civilization the artist is a pariah.

I have been speaking of normal or public education, but assuming that the would-be artist has survived this hazard and still persists in his desire to become an artist, he would then have the prospect of what is called 'art education'. This can be the worst hazard of all, and a great many are slaughtered in these academic abattoirs. The conflict between tradition and individual talent (which is the basic conflict in all forms of social adjustment) is now narrowed down to the problem of personal expression, and the would-be artist either has to accept the academic formulas, which may extend to style and treatment as well as to more technical questions of materials and methods of composition, or to assert his own vision. Success or failure may depend on the resolution of this conflict. If the authority of the academy is supreme, as it was in Europe throughout the seventeenth and eighteenth centuries, then success depends on the acceptance and exploitation of the academic formulas. Naturally an unintelligent repetition of these formulas will not lead to success: the artist must understand their purpose and may even subtly modify them to satisfy his personal taste. But to ignore them altogether is to incur neglect. A good illustration from the history of English art is provided by the contrast between the ideals and fortunes of Sir Joshua Reynolds and his contemporary William Blake. Reynolds was by no means a narrow-minded pedant; on the contrary, he was a man of broad sympathies and 'sweet reasonableness', and his own great reputation as a painter, not only in his own time but in the judgement of posterity, makes him an admirable example for the purpose of this discussion. That his success was due to self-imposed limitations—his realization that he had no gift for poetical compositions in the grand manner, but must confine himself to the interpretation of character—only adds to the interest and significance of his case. He has been accused of not practising what he preached (in his *Discourses*), but as Roger Fry pointed out in his edition of the *Discourses* (London, 1905), 'the notion that Reynolds as a critic ought to have bound himself within the limits of his own talent as an artist, that he was to recommend others to do no more than he had done himself, is palpably absurd. It is just because he had the gift, an unusual one among artists, of rising to a general view of art as a whole, and of regarding his own performance with objective impartiality, that he is so remarkable as a critic'.

If we turn to the *Discourses* we find Reynolds recommending that 'an implicit obedience to the *Rules of Art*, as established by the practice of the great Masters, should be exacted from the young students. That those models, which have passed through the approbation of ages, should be considered by them as perfect and infallible guides, as subjects for their imitation, not their criticism!' And he adds:

> 'I am confident that this is the only efficacious method of making a progress in the Arts; and that he who sets out with doubting, will find life finished before he becomes master of the rudiments. For it may be laid down as a maxim, that he who begins by presuming on his own sense, has ended his studies as soon as he had commenced them. Every opportunity, therefore, should be taken to discountenance that false and vulgar opinion, that rules are the fetters of genius; they are fetters only to men of no genius; as that armour, which upon the strong is an ornament and a defence, upon the weak and misshapen becomes a load, and cripples the body which it was made to protect.'

That Reynolds had the excellence of the art of painting at

heart rather than his own social success is not to be doubted, but again and again he points out that 'labour is the only price of *solid fame*', meaning by labour a patient following of the precepts of the Academy, and by solid fame social success. Nevertheless, towards the end of his *Discourses* he had the generosity to admit that by exception a man like Gainsborough might arrive at excellence (if not worldly success) in avoiding these precepts—'he found out a way of his own to accomplish his purpose'. But he warned his listeners against following this example, and in the eloquent conclusion to the *Discourses* he once more affirms that the greatest success in art cannot be obtained by any other means than great labour. Even Michelangelo, who 'might make the greatest pretensions to the efficacy of native genius and inspiration'—even Michelangelo, as he himself said of Raphael, 'did not possess his art from nature, but by long study'.

About 1808, thirty years after they were delivered, Blake wrote some annotations in his copy of the *Discourses* which showed the reaction of native genius to such a man as Reynolds and to his precepts. 'This man,' he declared, 'was fired by Satan to depress art,' and Blake had 'nothing but indignation and resentment' to express as he read the discourses of one who had been 'applauded and rewarded by the rich and great'. 'I consider Reynolds's *Discourses* to the Royal Academy as the simulations of the hypocrite who smiles particularly where he means to betray. His praise of Rafael is like the hysteric smile of revenge. His softness and candour, the hidden trap and poisoned feast. He praises Michelangelo for qualities which Michelangelo abhorred, and he blames Rafael for the only qualities which Rafael valued'—there is much more vituperation of this kind, about forty pages of it, but apart from a defence of Blake's own style in painting (delineation as against chiaroscuro) they return again and again to two themes: tradition and individual talent, and patronage. Reynolds 'mocked' inspiration and vision ('then and now, and I hope will always remain, my element, my eternal dwelling place') and he rigged the market in favour of his own kind of art—'the rich men of England form themselves into a society to sell and not to buy pictures. The artist who does not throw his contempt on such trading exhibitions, does not know either his own interest or his duty . . . The inquiry in England is not whether a man has talents and genius, but whether he is passive and polite and a virtuous ass and obedient to noblemen's opinions in art and science. If he is, he is a good man. If not, he must be starved.'

It may seem that this quarrel between Reynolds and Blake is irrelevant to the secret of success in art today. It is true that in some countries the academies of the eighteenth century no longer exercise the same degree of power, but they still have power among the bourgeoisie, and an artist's election to the academy usually carries with it social and economic success. Success, of course, is an ambiguous concept, and we must always distinguish, as the French do, between un *succès d'estime* and un *succès fou*. But what both Reynolds and Blake are saying is that success is largely dependent on personal qualities—labour in the one case, inspiration in the other. Assuming the possession of innate sensibility, we might conclude that each quality leads to a different kind of success, but unfortunately the artist of solid fame will always envy the inspiration of the native genius, while the native and untutored genius will always envy the solid fame of the artist who has succeeded by the assiduous cultivation of a modest talent.

Another personal factor in achieving success, almost as important as genius or long study, is what we might call charm (though some artists can exploit a reputation for being 'difficult'—anti-charm). This quality is perhaps too obvious to be worth mentioning, but from one's own observation of the world of art one sees what a difference an artist's personality can make. It is not merely an ability to establish easy relationships with his fellow-artists, with dealers and collectors, museum directors and critics. All this is more likely to help the second-rate artist than the great artist, who can afford to ignore such refinements (as Michelangelo did, or Gauguin). But since man's character is his destiny, it does follow that the public image of an artist will be formed, not only on the objective evidence of his work, but on the social impact of his behaviour. There is no surer road to success than the creation of a legend: the part played by their romantic, erratic, or merely distressing lives in the success (alas, for the most part posthumous) of artists like Gauguin, Van Gogh, Modigliani, Utrillo, cannot be ignored. But a legend *grows*: it cannot be deliberately created, though some artists, who lack other means to success, sometimes make the attempt. A legend, we might say, is not created without suffering (*malheur*): very different are those reputations which are the product of skilful publicity. The 'stunt', such as practised in our time so successfully by Salvador Dali and Georges Mathieu, is art redeemed by the arts of publicity.

The function of publicity must, of course, be taken seriously by the contemporary artist, if only because he is part of an economic system that functions through this medium (the situation is somewhat different in the communist system, but let us exclude this complication for the moment). The life of an artist in the capitalist world must be largely pre-occupied with the problems of exhibition and sale. A very complex sales organization now exists, largely in the hands of private dealers but not excluding artists' societies, which are co-operative sales organizations usually for the benefit of artists who have not yet acquired sufficient reputation to attract the interest of a dealer. Sales to collectors do still take place directly without the intermediary of a dealer; but it is often a condition of the contract between an artist and a dealer that all sales should pass through the dealer's hands—an arrangement which saves the artist a lot of trouble and secures a uniform scale of prices.

Dealers have their own methods of promotion and publicity

and the success of these may determine the success of the artist. There is no exact correspondence between the quality of the art and the success of the artist; as in any other competitive sphere, it is possible to sell an inferior product by superior sales organization—an organization that may extend to every wile of the advertising profession. Works of art are now as subject to skilful promotion as cosmetics or cigarettes. The success that comes from such methods is, however, always subject to independent criticism, and that is why the existence of organs of independent criticism, and of incorruptible critics, is so essential in our time. It should be impossible in questions of taste to fool all the public all the time, but in fact, once an artist has become fashionable by clever methods of publicity, it takes many years of patient criticism to destroy his false reputation—so few people read serious criticism.

The rôle of fashion, if that can be separated from the methods of publicity, is inexplicable. There are cases of artists who, without any preparatory publicity, and without any claim to greatness, have suddenly become successful overnight. Their works are shown in a gallery for the first time, and without any lead from the critics or any persuasion from publicity, they immediately sell. (Much more common, of course, is the case of the artist whose work is well received by the critics, well advertised, but completely fails to attract the public.) One can only suppose that the artist in this case has by chance satisfied some repressed need in the collective unconscious—there is exactly the same phenomenon in literature, the novel which, for inexplicable reasons, becomes a best-seller.

The element of chance therefore plays a considerable part in the achievement of success—far more than a rational critic like Sir Joshua Reynolds would allow. But this is to consider only happy chances; the phenomenon also has its negative aspects. The lack of success during their lifetimes of many artists who are posthumously recognized may be due to personal qualities of diffidence, as I have already suggested, or to incompetent methods of salesmanship, but it may be just bad luck. Apart from the bad luck of being born in a remote province, or a small country (chances which afflict the poet much more severely than the painter); apart from the bad luck of being born to poverty or with physical defects (such as bad eyesight), there is an element of fatality in any artist's career which cannot be controlled. So much depends, in what is at all times a game of chance, upon the people we meet and the places we visit. Many artists have recorded the decisive importance of some strange meeting, of some personal influence that came into their lives with transforming effect. The impact of Masaccio on Fra Angelico is perhaps the typical example. The development of colonialism during the nineteenth century and the consequent importation of an hitherto unknown type of art—the tribal sculpture of Africa and Oceania—is an example from the modern period.

There is one further element which we must now take into account, the most impalpable of all—the *Zeitgeist*. This is a German concept which has been taken over by the rest of the world and I will not presume to define it for a German audience. Partly it is the question of fashion which I have already dealt with, but fashion is an epiphenomenon, confined to limited circles and of limited duration. The Zeitgeist is something that pervades a whole epoch and penetrates all its intellectual manifestations. There is no escaping it, but nevertheless some artists are less subject to its influence than others and these are often the greatest artists. I have already mentioned Blake, and as a poet rather than a visual artist he is as good an example as could be found anywhere. A comparable German poet is Hölderlin, but perhaps he had more sympathetic understanding from the carpenter, Zimmer, with whom he lived during the long years of his madness, than from contemporaries like Goethe and Schiller. In the plastic arts Hans von Marées is a typical case. Indeed, it is generally true, as Wordsworth said, that an original artist has to create the audience that can appreciate his work. In every artist there is a proselytizer.

Finally there is a general sociological problem which is particularly serious in democratic societies and for which, within the general concept of democracy, there is no obvious solution. Success in art, as in any other field of activity, implies distinction, and in a capitalist society, it implies relative wealth. It is indeed one of the anomalies of communist society, as it has evolved in Russia and China, that the very concept of artist implies an *élite*, and artists in these communist societies enjoy, not only a higher status, but privileges of many kinds, not excluding financial ones. It is true that, especially in China, these privileges have to be enjoyed modestly and unobtrusively, but nevertheless they exist.

This problem was recognized by the greatest democratic sociologist of our time, Karl Mannheim. He saw it as a special case of the general problem of reconciling 'freedom' (which the artist needs if he is to function as an artist) with the democratic ideal of 'equality'. In general terms the solution lies in giving art an organic function within the life of the community. Mannheim recognized the dangers implicit in the concept of *art engagé* (socialist realism, propaganda art, etc.) but he thought that the opposite extreme of *l'art pour l'art* was equally dangerous. In the nineteenth century, for example, 'the social position of a large section of the intellectual *élite* was that of the bohemian, without corporate ties, without a well-defined place in society; the members of this group lived in a curious milieu in which self-styled or genuine men of genius were thrown together with black sheep from aristocratic or bourgeois families, *déclassé* drifters, prostitutes, matinee idols, and other fugitives from organized society. . . . All this exerted a considerable influence upon their thinking. . . . Such intellectuals will cultivate a set of values far removed from the concerns of ordinary people.'

Mannheim was optimistic enough to think that this situation could be changed in a democratic society, not by making the artist a propagandist or a politically conscious individual, but by a process of 'integration', which, however, he does not define in detail. He merely assumes that 'as democratization progresses, the ties between the intellectual strata and society at large are likely to become closer and more organic. This need not mean that art will become crudely propagandist, but only that it will have a more organic function in life than *l'art pour l'art* had.'

These words were written in 1933, but the *Demokratisierung des Geistes* to which Mannheim looked forward has nowhere been manifest in the democratic world. Instead art has become more and more abstruse and esoteric, more and more removed from the concerns of ordinary people. To call this development the cult of *l'art pour l'art* does not solve the problem, and is not a scientific diagnosis of a phenomenon now so universal and so spiritually significant as abstract art. One can explain abstract art in sociological terms—as the art of a civilization alienated from nature and from organic processes of production—but this merely means that a democratic industrial society has produced an appropriate type of art. Mannheim indeed recognized that 'there is an intrinsic correlation between the increasing abstractness of the symbols used in communication, and the democratic character of the culture. Élites which are not impelled to make their knowledge generally accessible will not engage in formalization, analysis, and articulation. They will content themselves, either with unanalysed intuition, or with sacred knowledge reserved for an *élite* and handed down among its members *en bloc*.'

The artist in the modern democratic society, Mannheim thought, would gradually surrender his esotericism because in such a society there is a tendency to bar qualitative elements from its experience in favour of greater communicability. But this is not what has happened in the Western World; on the contrary, and in spite of the spread of information through media like television and the film, there is an increasing divorce between art, which increases in concreteness and self-sufficiency, and those media of communication, such as film, television and the Press, which communicated through popular images. The result is that there are today two distinct criteria of success: the *succès d'estime* which is confined to an *élite* (albeit an *élite* of considerable dimensions) and success among the literate masses which is conveyed through quite different media of communication. The necessity of using these ugly neologisms (*élite*, mass, media of communication) is an indication of the unprecedented nature of this cultural situation. Mannheim's hope or belief that these criteria would eventually merge together, that quantitative judgements would supersede qualitative judgements in a democratic society, is really a confession that the aristocratic ideals of fine art have no place in an egalitarian democracy. It is a conclusion that was reached, on different grounds, by both Nietzsche and Burckhardt; it is a dilemma that today presents us with its naked and unresolved contradictions.

9

THE FREEDOM OF THE ARTIST

> The bourgeois believe that liberty consists in absence of social organization; that liberty is a negative quality, a deprivation of existing obstacles to it; and not a positive quality, the reward of endeavour and wisdom. . . . Because of this basic fallacy this type of intellectual always tries to cure positive social evils, such as wars, by negative individual actions, such as non-co-operation, passive resistance or conscientious objection. This is because he cannot rid himself of the assumption that the individual is free. But we have shown that the individual is never free. He can only obtain freedom by social co-operation. He can only do what he wants by using social forces. . . . But in order to use social relations he must understand them. He must become conscious of the laws of society, just as, if he wants to lever up a stone, he must know the laws of levers.
>
> Christopher Caudwell, *Studies in a Dying Culture* (1938).

One of the most obvious generalizations from the history of art is to the effect that at various times in the past different conceptions of the technique and content of art have prevailed, but that in their time these conceptions were always regarded as the normal mode of expression. To the degree that we are aware of this relativity in standards, we shall accept as perfectly natural and inevitable that the peculiar social conditions of our time should give rise to an original style of art. That possibility being granted, we might further regard it as also perfectly natural that there should be a time-lag in public appreciation, and that the new form of art should find itself in opposition to the traditions inherited from the immediate past. But the special character of the contemporary situation is that there is not an art which we can call specifically modern, but at least four styles of art which make that claim. We have in the first place the specifically modern styles best defined by the words *superrealism* and *constructivism*, styles which, the more logically they develop, the more incompatible with one another they seem to become. But to complete the picture of art today, we must be prepared to admit the independent existence of two further styles: *realism* and *expressionism*.

By realism we mean that style of art which attempts to represent the objective reality of the external world. The word 'realism' can be used in a narrower sense, to indicate a style of art that concentrates on scenes of low life, or on morbid or horrible details, but that is not a very logical use of the term. Realism is also confused with naturalism, but that word either means the same as realism, and is therefore unnecessary, or it indicates something more restricted than realism—that aspect of the world we habitually identify as 'nature': trees, flowers, landscape generally, and even human nature. In spite of its ambiguity, realism is the right philosophical term to describe that whole school of art, in literature as well as in the plastic arts, which endeavours to give an exact representation of the external or objective world, or rather, of select details of that world.

Expressionism, too, is based on the observation of the external world, but it no longer pretends to be objective. It admits that the recording instrument, the artist, is a sensitive or subjective element, and it suggests that his view of the world is necessarily affected by his emotional reaction to what he sees. The expressionist artist may believe in the existence of an objective reality; but that reality is merely hypothetical, and the real reality, the only reality which the artist can faithfully record, is the sensation provoked in his mind by this external agent. A camera, he would say, may conceivably record the external features of Sir Winston Churchill; but that is not the Winston Churchill I apprehend with my senses, nor has it any correspondence to the emotional reactions which take place whenever I become aware of Sir Winston Churchill. If I paint what I see and at the same time feel, it will not be like a camera portrait of Sir Winston Churchill: it will be more like what would be called a caricature of him. It will, in short, be expressive rather than realistic.

If we divide art into these four groups then I think we shall find that they cover all the manifestations of artistic activity taking place today, and indeed, all the manifestations that have ever taken place in the past. The only peculiarity about the situation today is that all four types of artistic activity tend to take place at the same time, whereas in the past the emphasis has tended to be on one or other of the four types to the exclusion of the other three. What I think it is still necessary to realize is that all four types of activity are natural, and that indeed they correspond exactly to four types of mental activity which have a long traditional history, and which have been revived by modern psychology.

The human mind is not a region which can be charted with any exactitude, but psychologists have resorted to certain schematic representations that help to give us a clear picture of what is an obscure and complex reality. The particular formula which we should find most useful is that elaborated in great detail by Jung, but actually, as Jung acknowledges in his book on *Psychological Types*, the main areas and boundaries have been gradually evolved by the general science of psychology. Here[1] we do not need to go much beyond these accepted commonplaces, which make a distinction between four primary functions of the mind—four activities or faculties which co-exist in the mind of every individual and which we call Thinking, Feeling, Intuition and Sensation.

Now, though it is conceivable that the mind is capable of states of pure thought, pure feeling, pure sensation and pure intuition, most of its activity is of a mixed nature, and takes place between these cardinal points. Thus, thought passes imperceptibly into intuitive thought, which we call speculation, then through intuition into intuitive feeling, through feeling into sensory feeling, through sensation into sensory thinking (or what we call empirical thought), and so back to thinking. But in any individual, one or the other of the four primary functions of the mind will tend to predominate, and according to Jung and other psychologists, what we call the character of the individual—the psychological type to which he belongs—is determined by the particular balance established between the four primary functions.

The plastic arts are, of course, all expressed through the medium of sensation, but what they express is the mind or personality of the artist. If we can distinguish four types of mental personality, there should logically be four corresponding types of art—and we have already found that there are four such types. It only remains to identify each type of art with its corresponding psychological function, and this does not present any difficulty. A detailed demonstration of these correspondences involves psychological technicalities which would be out of place in the present general essay, and which in any case are of purely schematic value. For it must be repeatedly emphasized that there are no exact limits between these divisions of mind

[1] I have discussed the subject in greater detail in Education Through Art, especially in a chapter on 'Temperament and Expression'.

and of art: they merge into one another, and between realism and constructivism, between constructivism and superrealism, between superrealism and expressionism, and finally between expressionism and realism, we get intermediate types of art which fuse thought and intuition, intuition and feeling, feeling and sensation, or sensation and thought.

I have only introduced this psychological comparison to make clear what I consider to be the most striking achievement of modern art—an achievement of which it is not yet conscious. Modern art has broken through the artificial boundaries and limitations which we owe to a one-sided and prejudiced view of the human personality. Modern psychology has shown that the mind of man is complex; that it is a balance of forces—of various impulses or unconscious 'drives', and that the various psychological types into which human beings can be divided are determined by the predominance of one particular impulse or group of impulses. What I am saying, therefore, is simple enough and should always have been admitted: namely, that there is not one type of art to which all types of men should conform, but as many types of art as there are types of men; and that the categories into which we divide art should naturally correspond to the categories into which we divide men. This statement does not exclude the philosophical problem of *value*, to which I shall come presently; I am not suggesting that there is no possibility of making judgements about the various types of art, or of man. But from a scientific point of view, each type of art is the legitimate expression of a type of mental personality. From a scientific point of view, that is to say, realism and idealism, expressionism and constructivism are all natural phenomena, and the warring schools into which men divide themselves are merely the products of ignorance and prejudice. A true eclecticism can and should enjoy all the manifestations of the creative impulse in man.

If we could imagine a society in which each individual pursued his course in independence, happily producing what he wished to produce without interference from his neighbours, then in such a community each type of artist could express himself in the manner which he found most apt. Constructivists and superrealists, realists and expressionists, could live and work side by side in perfect amity. I do not suggest that such a community of individuals is too idealistic to contemplate; it is, in fact, the ideal towards which we should aim. But actually, here and now, we live in communities of a very different character. All the various societies which together make up modern civilization are in fact highly organized and complex, and according to their type of organization they encourage a particular type of art, or even discourage all types of art.

Modern societies can be divided into two general types—democratic and totalitarian. It is true that you might find, in India or the Pacific Ocean, a small state which still represented a different conception of society—feudal or communist—but such societies are vestigial. The general drift of modern economic forces compels society in general to adopt one or other of the complex and highly organized forms which we call democratic and totalitarian. In theory, the distinction between these two forms is very sharp—indeed, it is so irreconcilable that it has led repeatedly to deathly conflict. In practice, and particularly under the stress of war, there is a tendency for the two forms to approximate—the totalitarian making concessions of liberty in the interests of morale, the democratic elaborating a centralized control in the interests of immediate efficiency and power. In the present context therefore, it would be better to abandon the ambiguous word 'democracy' and to present the contrast in irreconcilable terms—totalitarian and libertarian.

The broad distinction between the totalitarian and the libertarian state is that society in the former is a planned organization to which all the constitutent individuals or units are forcibly subordinated, whilst in the latter, society is the result of the free co-operation of individuals for their common benefit. The totalitarian state has the apparent advantage of efficiency, but by killing individual initiative it tends to make the state an inelastic, inorganic and anti-vital machine. The libertarian state is haphazard, apparently inefficient, certainly exasperating to men with tidy minds, but we claim that, like nature itself, though wasteful, it does live and let live, and that, above all, it allows for the development of individual sensibility and intelligence.

Accepting these facts, what we would then *a priori* expect does in fact occur. The two most completely totalitarian states, China[2] and Russia, are precisely the states in which the realistic style in art not merely prevails, but *is made* to prevail. It is the official and definitive style, to which all artists within the state must conform. All other styles are banned, and the artists who practise them are persecuted. It is interesting to note that this ban is applied, not merely to superrealism and expressionism, which might be supposed to have some socially disintegrating effects, but also to constructivism, the aim of which is so positive and tectonic. People who exalt the rational motive above all others inevitably and instinctively reject any activity that proceeds from another region of the mind.

In the case of the democratic state, we are not able to make any such neat *a priori* identification—and for a very good reason. The libertarian attitude is essentially an experimental attitude, and therefore in the field of art it welcomes any form of activity that will provide a working hypothesis. The American philosopher, John Dewey, has identified democracy and the scientific method. Let me quote a few relevant sentences from his book, *Freedom and Culture*:[3]

---

[2] Not completely in China; there a good deal of artistic liberty shelters (as I observed when I visited the country in 1959) under the cover of 'tradition'.

[3] London (Allen & Unwin), 1940, p. 102.

'It is of the nature of science not so much to tolerate as to welcome diversity of opinion, while it insists that inquiry brings the evidence of observed facts to bear to effect a consensus of conclusions—and even then to hold the conclusion subject to what is ascertained and made public in further new inquiries. I would not claim that any existing democracy has ever made complete or adequate use of scientific method in deciding upon its policies. But freedom of inquiry, toleration of diverse views, freedom of communication, the distribution of what is found out to every individual as the ultimate intellectual consumer, are involved in the democratic as in the scientific method. When democracy openly recognizes the existence of *problems* and the need for probing them *as* problems as its glory, it will relegate political groups that pride themselves upon refusing to admit incompatible opinions to the obscurity which already is the fate of similar groups in science'.

Similarly, I feel inclined to say that when such a society, which must therefore be a libertarian society, openly recognizes the existence of distinct types of personality, and the necessity for these types to express themselves artistically, it will relegate artistic groups that pride themselves upon refusing to admit incompatible styles to the obscurity which is already the fate of similar groups in science. Any kind of exclusiveness or intolerance is just as opposed to the principles of liberty as social exclusiveness or political intolerance. In this respect art, and all cultural modes of expression, are of exactly the same status as political opinions.

The scientific method implies, nevertheless, some progress and some definite conclusions. The progress may be slow and the conclusions may be tentative, but at some stage the problem seems to be solved and a certain line of action to be indicated. It is only in chess, in the crossword puzzle and sometimes in mathematics, that the problem is set for the mere sake of arriving at a solution. The organization of society has, therefore, or should have, a definite aim, and though that aim may be described in general terms as the achievement of the good life, the greatest happiness of the greatest number, and so on, from time to time it has a more specific aim—or rather, this general aim is divided into many detailed aims—shorter stages towards the final achievement. At the present moment most of these aims are subordinated to the one aim of defending our liberty from the threat of the totalitarian power of Russia, but in more normal times we have various social and cultural aims, some of which impinge very directly on the province of the artist. It is precisely because these aims are *various* that they will demand, not one type of artist, but all types. Let me try to indicate briefly the possible ways in which each type of artist might find his function in a libertarian society of the future.

A democracy does not despise or suppress that faculty which the totalitarian socialist makes so exclusive—his thinking or rational faculty. The libertarian socialist must also plan, but his plans, apart from being tentative and experimental, will make the widest use of all human faculties. Thus, he will plan the building of a new city, or the rebuilding of an old one. But in so doing he will not merely consider the rational factors, such as the distribution of the buildings, the width and direction of the streets, the provision of open spaces and recreational amenities, all of which can be arrived at by the process of thought; he will also consider the relation of mass to mass, of surface to surface, of line and outline, until he has reached, through the faculty of intuition, a natural harmony. But even that is not sufficient. The libertarian planner must also remember that cities are built for citizens, and that the houses and buildings will be inhabited, not by ciphers, but by human beings with sensations and feelings, and that these human beings will be unhappy unless they can freely express themselves in their environment. It may be that these faculties can only be expressed individually, or in group activities like drama and sport; but at least your city must be so planned that it allows for the possibility of such activities. No doubt the planner will remember to provide a theatre and a sports-ground; what he is likely to forget is some provision for the retirement and seclusion of each person. For it is upon personal happiness that society ultimately and collectively depends.

It is, still more certainly, upon personal happiness that the future of art depends. But by 'happiness' I do not mean that state of eupeptic contentment which is actually of all states of mind the one least favourable to the production of a work of art. Happiness, in the field of art, means work: the capacity and ability to create something near the heart's desire. The happiness is not in the possession of the thing created, but in the act of creating it. It is the thesis so often and so rightly defended by Eric Gill—the thesis 'that human culture is the natural product of human living, and that human living is naturally and chiefly a matter of human working; that leisure is in its essence recreative, that the object of recreation is to fit us for living, that we may rejoice as a giant to run the course.' We make a table and call it work; we make a picture and call it art if we mean to sell the picture, recreation if we make it for our own amusement. But there is really no distinction: the art is not determined by the purpose of the thing we make, but by its inherent qualities, the qualities with which the artist has endowed it; and the pleasure of art comes from the act of creating these and, in a secondary and stimulating way, from the mental act of re-creating them in contemplation. What I wish to prevent is any narrow conception either of the artist or of the work of art. Every human being is potentially an artist, and this potentiality is of considerable social significance. The individual and society are the opposite poles of a very complex relationship. The individual is anti-social at the time of birth—observe the early days of any baby. He only becomes social by a painful process of adaptation, during which he acquires what we call, paradoxically, his personality, but actually that compromise character which is the result of sub-ordinating personality to the prevalent conception of social normality. The psychological ills from which human beings suffer are a product of this compromise, or maladjustment. What becomes more and more certain is that these ills can to a large extent be avoided by the practice of an art. The people who make things—I have no evidence beyond my own observation—seem to be less liable to nervous breakdowns, and one of the recognized forms of treatment for mental diseases is known as 'occupational therapy'. No one would suggest that the function of art is merely to keep people healthy; but it has its subjective effect. The artist not only creates an object external to himself: in doing so he also vitally reorganizes the balance of impulses within himself.

Our glance at the social function of art therefore reinforces the libertarian conception of art. All types of art are not merely permissible, but desirable. The needs of society comprise, not only the outward structure of a world to live in, but also the inward structure of a mind capable of enjoying life. We must therefore search for methods of encouraging the artist—the artist latent in each one of us.

There still remains the question of *value* in art. We may all become artists, but unless our human nature changes radically, only a few of us can become *great* artists. How do we measure this difference—the difference between mediocrity and genius?

The truth is, there is not one measure, but several. Some people, and possibly the majority of people at some time, use one only of these measures; others use a combination of two or more measures and take their average. Actually I find that these measures are again four in number. There is first the direct application of what we call a canon—that is to say, an established law. It may be a law of geometrical proportion, of colour combinations, of a definite type of human figure, of a definite 'order' or 'module' in architecture. It is a measure we are conscious of, and can apply exactly. Then—and this is the measure that has been most used in the past century—there is the measure of sensibility. The human being is regarded as a sensitive instrument who gives out and receives delicate vibrations in the presence of colours, textures and spatial relations, and a work of art is measured by the number and intensity of the vibrations which emanate from him. Nearly related to this kind of sensibility, but in reality quite distinct, is our intuitive apprehension of space and time, and our expression of their relations in rhythm and harmony: our intuition of the absolute values of form. Finally, there is our appreciation of the dramatic or symbolic significance of the pictorial content of a work of art—the feelings which are aroused in us by the images that the artist uses to express himself.

We have thus four methods of critical approach to the work of art, and each method is valid for its corresponding type of art. Between these critical poles there will again be mixed modes of apprehension and judgement, so that the satisfaction we derive from the observance of academic canons can be modified on the one side by our intuition of harmonic relations, and on the other side by our sensibility to colours and textures. At the other extreme the psychological significance of our dramatic images may be combined with a sensitive rendering of these images, and even by an 'abstraction' of such images; in other words, superrealism will merge, as we know it does, towards constructivism on the one side and towards expressionism on the other. But again I think it will be found that the opposite points of the compass tend to conflict—we cannot, that is to say, at one and the same time satisfy the very rational and conscious laws of an academic canon and express the fantasies which we find ready-made in the unconscious. Nor do I think that the extreme sensibility which we get in the impressionistic paintings of Monet or Renoir can combine with the formal intuitions which are the basis of the art of Seurat or Ben Nicholson. But the mind of the spectator has more than one mode of appreciation—more than one approach to art—and I find nothing reprehensible—indeed I find it but natural—that one man's taste should be universal. Art, like the human mind itself, embraces contradictions; it is the balance of these contradictions that produces the high degree of tension necessary for the production of the greatest works of art.

Actually we each tend to select the critical approach appropriate to the psychological type to which we belong. Whether the wholly harmonious mind exists—the mind equally balanced between thought and feeling, between intuition and sensation—is perhaps doubtful, but surely that is the ideal towards which we ought to strive. Only such a mind can appreciate the fullness and richness of life. If we come to the conclusion that this complete and harmonious being cannot exist in our modern form of society, then our aim should be to change that form of society until such a life becomes possible. In this great aim, in which the energies of humanity will be absorbed for centuries to come, a right understanding of the nature of art and of the function of the artist is fundamental.

10

THE NATURE OF REVOLUTIONARY ART

> Like industry, art has never adapted itself to the demands of theorists; it always upsets their plans of social harmony, and humanity has found the freedom of art far too satisfactory ever to think of allowing it to be controlled by the creators of dull systems of sociology. The Marxists are accustomed to seeing the ideologists look at things the wrong way round, and so, in contrast to their enemies, they should look upon art as a reality which begets ideas and not as an application of ideas.
>
> Georges Sorel, *Reflections on Violence*.

In the fragmentary notes which conclude his Introduction to *The Critique of Political Economy*, Marx recognized 'an unequal relationship between the development of material production and artistic production', but did not despair of reconciling such a contradiction by means of the dialectical method. He himself never had the time or opportunity to resolve the problem, and some of his remarks on the subject are in the nature of hasty generalizations which no doubt he would have corrected on further consideration—as, for example, his explanation of the eternal appeal of Greek art as due to the eternal child in us, an hypothesis evidently derived directly from Vico. Marx's hesitation and, indeed, faltering over this problem should at least have deterred his followers from a superficial treatment of one of the most complex categories of history that still await dialectical analysis. This immense subject does not concern us now, but on the basis of a superficial and essentially undialectical approach to the whole problem, certain assumptions have been made as to the nature of a true revolutionary art, or a true proletarian art, which only bring ridicule on the cultural aspects of the revolutionary movement.

Revolutionary art should be revolutionary. That surely is a simple statement from which we can begin the discussion. We can at once dismiss the feeble interpretation of such a statement as an injunction to paint pictures of red flags, hammers and sickles, factories and machines, or revolutionary subjects in general. (If I take examples from the plastic arts, I do so only for convenience, and what I say would apply equally to music[1] and poetry and all the arts we are concerned with.) But such a feeble interpretation does actually persist among communists, and is responsible for the partisan adulation of a competent but essentially second-rate artist like Diego Rivera.

We can best approach the question from the angle of an abstract art like architecture. (That this particular art has undergone some queer transformations in Russia is beside the point; there are explanations of the anomaly, but they have little to do

---

[1] A pathetic moral may be drawn from the development of the composer Shostakovitch. An excellent analysis of the progressive deterioration of this artist under political pressure was made by Gerald Abraham in *Horizon*, vol. vi, no. 33 (September 1942). The 'pressure' may not be overtly political: it may be the politician's interpretation of popular taste, which is rather worse, for then the politician is presuming to make and enforce an aesthetic judgement. Cf. Emma Lu Davis, quoted on pp. 75–6 above.

with aesthetics.) Architecture is a necessary art, and it is intimately bound up with the social reconstruction which must take place under a revolutionary régime. How do we, as Englishmen, conceive a revolutionary architecture? As a reversion to Tudor rusticity, or Georgian stateliness, or the bourgeois pomp of the neo-classical style? Surely none of these styles can for a moment be considered in relation to the city of the future. Must we not rather confidently look forward to a development of that architecture which, in Walter Gropius's words, 'bodies itself forth, not in stylistic imitation or ornamental frippery, but in those simple and sharply modelled designs in which every part merges naturally into the comprehensive volume of the whole'? Only in this manner, by following the path clearly indicated by Gropius and his followers, can we find 'a concrete expression of the life of our epoch'.

That surely must be admitted. If we then pass from architecture and ask ourselves what is the parallel to this new style in the arts of painting and sculpture, can we for a moment be satisfied with a Rivera or a Tsapline? Is there not rather an essential contradiction between such anecdotal and 'literary' art and the vitality and intellectual strength of the new architecture?

The question cannot be answered without a short digression on the nature of art. Any considerable work of art has two distinct elements: a formal element appealing to our sensibility for reasons which cannot be stated with any clarity, but which are certainly psychological if not physiological in origin; and an arbitrary or variable element of more complex appeal which like a suit of clothing seems to cover these underlying forms. It is at least arguable that the purely formal element in art does not change; that the same canons of harmony and proportion are present in primitive art, in Greek art, in Gothic art, in Renaissance art and in the art of the present day. Such forms, we may say, are archetypal; due to the physical structure of the world and the psychological structure of man. And it is for this reason that the artist, with some show of reason, can take up an attitude of detachment. It is his sense of the importance of the archetypal which makes him relatively indifferent to the phenomenal.

The recognition of such universal formal qualities in art is consistently materialistic. It no more contradicts the materialistic interpretation of history than does a recognition of the relative permanency of the human form, or of the forms of crystals in geology. Certain factors in life are constant; but to that extent they are not part of history. History is concerned with that part of life which is subject to change; and the Marxian dialectic is an interpretation of history, not a theory of the biological structure or morphology of life.

If the critic of formalism will grant the existence of permanent and unchanging elements in art, then it can be admitted that at various periods there has been a different valuation of such elements. In fact, what is the difference between classical and romantic epochs but a difference in the emphasis given to the formal basis of works of art? We cannot say that a romantic painter like Delacroix lacks form—or that a classical painter like Poussin has too much of it. If we could in any way measure the degree of form in these two artists we should probably find that it was equal.

But in the classical artist the form is so important that the subject-matter is almost irrelevant; whilst in the romantic artist the subject-matter is so important that it completely overwhelms the form. It is merely, we might say, a difference of accent. But it is in precisely such a way that a reasonable Marxist would expect art to be inflected. We can, therefore, in any broad historical generalization, dismiss the underlying formal structure of art, to concentrate on style and mannerism. For it is in style and mannerism that the prevailing ideology of a period is expressed.

If we admit so much, it follows that it is a mere illusion for the artist to imagine that he can for ever maintain an attitude of detachment. I can only see one logical exception—the artist who can so deprive his work of temporary and accidental qualities that what he achieves is in effect pure form. And, significantly enough, that is the claim of one extreme of the abstract or constructivist movement, an extreme which includes some of the most talented artists now living. Having no sympathy with any existing ideology, they attempt to escape into a world without ideologies. They shut themselves within the Ivory Tower, and it is just possible that, for the time being (the very special time in which we live), their tactics may be of some advantage to the art of the future. Their position will become clearer as we proceed.

Apart from such a desperate retreat, we have to admit that the artist cannot in any effective way avoid the economic conditions of his time; he cannot ignore them, for they will not ignore him. Reality, in one guise or another, forces the artist along a determined course, and if the artist does not realize this, it is only because he is in the middle of the stream, where the water is deep and the current strong.

As I have said elsewhere,[2] this question of the relation of the individual to the collective society of which he is a member is the fundamental issue, in art as well as in politics. It is the fundamental question within religion too, for what is the Reformation but the affirmation of the autocentric will of the individual against the collective rule of the Church? Philosophically it is the issue between Scholasticism and Cartesianism, between materialism and idealism. But the relation between mind and reality, between the individual and the community, is not one of precedence; it is more one of action and reaction, a process of tacking against the wind. The current of reality is strong, and troubles the mind; but the mind embraces this contrary force, and is lifted higher, and carried away farther, by the very opposition. And so with the individual and the community: complete freedom means inevitable decadence. The mind must feel an

---

[2] *Art and Society* (London: new edn, 1956).

opposition—must be tamped with hard realities if it is to have any blasting power.

That by no means exhausts the problem of the relation of the individual to society. It is a problem which in its psychological as well as sociological aspects I have discussed more thoroughly in another book,[3] and all I can say at present is that I think the relative freedom of the individual—I mean, of course, his intellectual freedom—can be justified within the Marxian orthodoxy. Stalin has said that 'Marxism starts out with the assumption that people's tastes and requirements are not, and cannot be, equal in quality or in quantity, either in the period of Socialism or in the period of Communism'. Tastes and requirements do not become differentiated in quality without independence of thought and criticism, and such independence is essential for any dialectical development in culture. The U.S.S.R. has found it necessary, purely for pragmatic reasons, to admit a certain degree of what is called 'self-criticism', thus recognizing a social rather than a political justification for intellectual freedom. The psychology of the individual cannot be separated from the psychology of the group, and for that reason alone the old conception of individuality will not serve for the new order of society.

Let us return to the actualities of modern art. Excluding the great mass of academic bourgeois art, and within the general category of revolutionary art, we have two distinct movements, both professing to be modern, both *intentionally* revolutionary.

The first of these has no very descriptive label, but is essentially formalist, in the sense already mentioned. It is sometimes called abstract, sometimes non-figurative, sometimes constructivist, sometimes geometric. It is most typically represented by painters like Kandinsky, Mondrian and Ben Nicholson; and by sculptors like Pevsner, Gabo and Barbara Hepworth.

---

[3] *Education Through Art* (London and New York: new edn, 1958).

The second movement has a distinctive name—*Surréalisme* or Superrealism—and is represented by painters like Max Ernst, Salvador Dali, Miró, Tanguy, and by a sculptor like Arp.

The first movement is plastic, objective and ostensibly non-political.

The second group is literary (even in paint), subjective, and is actively communist, though generally anti-Stalinist.

Those distinctions are obvious, on the surface. But I want to suggest that we cannot be satisfied with such superficial distinctions. We cannot accept the superrealists at their own valuation, and welcome them as the only true revolutionary artists. Nevertheless, they are performing a very important revolutionary function, and it must be said on their behalf that they realize the importance of their function with far more clarity than the official Marxians, who have shown them no favour. For official Marxians, concentrating on their economic problems, do not see the relevance of the cultural problem, more particularly the artistic problem. The mind of the artist, they complacently assume, that too will, in Trotsky's phrase, limp after the reality the politicians are creating.

But everywhere the greatest obstacle to the creation of this new social reality is the existence of the cultural heritage of the past—the religion, the philosophy, the literature and the art which makes up the whole complex ideology of the bourgeois mind. The logic of the facts—the economic facts: war, poverty amidst plenty, social injustice—that logic cannot be denied. But so long as the bourgeois mind has its bourgeois ideology it will deny the facts; it will construct an elaborate rationalization which effectively ignores them.

The superrealists, who possess very forceful expositors of their point of view, realize this very clearly, and the object of their movement is therefore to discredit the bourgeois ideology in art, to destroy the academic conception of art. Their whole tendency is negative and destructive. The particular method they adopt, in so far as they have a common method, consists in breaking down the barriers between the conscious reality of life and the unconscious reality of the dream-world—to so mingle fact and fancy that the normal concept of reality no longer has existence. It is a similar tendency which Carl Einstein found in the later work of Braque, and to some extent Braque may be considered as a superrealist—Picasso too. Superrealists like Ernst and Dali complete the disintegration of the academic concept of reality begun by Picasso and Braque.

We can see, therefore, the place of superrealism in the revolutionary movement. What of this other kind of modern art—the art of pure form immured in its Ivory Tower?

That art, too, I wish to contend, has its revolutionary function, and in the end it is the most important function of all. Super-realism is a negative art, as I have said, a destructive art; it follows that it has only a temporary rôle; it is the art of a transitional period. It may lead to a new romanticism, especially in literature, but that lies beyond its immediate function.

But abstract art has a positive function. It keeps inviolate, until such time as society will once more be ready to make use of them, the universal qualities of art—those elements which sur-vive all change and revolutions. It may be said that as such it is merely art in pickle—an activity divorced from reality, of no immediate interest to the revolutionary. But that, I maintain, is a very short view of the situation. Such art is not so much in pickle as might be supposed. For in one sphere, in architecture and to some extent in industrial art, it is already in social action. There we find the essential link between the abstract movement in modern painting and the most advanced movement in modern architecture—the architecture of Gropius, Mies van der Rohe, Frank Lloyd Wright, Aalto, Le Corbusier. . . . It is not merely a similarity of form and intention, but an actual and intimate association of personalities.

This single link points the way to the art of the future—the art of a classless society. It is impossible to predict all the forms of this art, and it will be many years before it reaches its maturity. But we cannot build a new society—and we must literally build such a society, with bricks and mortar, steel and glass—we cannot build such a society without artists. The artists are there, waiting for their opportunity: abstract artists who are, in this time of transition, perfecting their formal sensibility,[4] and who will be ready, when the time comes, to apply their talents to the great work of reconstruction. Reconstruction is not work for romantic traditionalists and literary sentimentalists. Constructive socialism is realistic, scientific, essentially classical. But let us realize that we have false romanticists in our midst—tender-minded idealists who would like to blur the precise outlines of our vision with sentimental ideals of naturalism, homespun simplicity and social naïvety, community-singing and what is now called 'pop' art. Such people imagine that revolutionary art is a kind of folk-art, peasant pottery, madrigals and ballads: the Russians encourage the debased lacquer and papier-mâché crafts of Palekh and Mstera, and their so-called 'socialist realism' is merely bourgeois pictorialism. We want a conception of art which is at once more imaginative and more precise, even intellectual and 'difficult', something which we can without falsity and self-deception put beside the great creative epochs of the past.

[4] I have dealt with the social function of the abstract artist in *Art and Industry* (London and New York, 1956).

11

THE PSYCHOLOGY OF REACTION

Reaction, and the ideology of reaction which we may call reactionaryism, is not confined to the arts. It is perhaps above all a political phenomenon, and as a matter of fact the reactionary artist is often found associating himself with a reactionary political party. Nevertheless, I propose to leave reactionary politics out of the present discussion, except in so far as an occasional reference may illuminate the same phenomenon in the arts.

As in politics, so in the arts, we must begin with a distinction, not always maintained, between reactionaryism and conservatism. Conservatism is a positive doctrine: it asserts that certain political institutions—the monarchy, for example—if not divinely ordained, are at least of absolute validity, and that all our efforts should be directed to maintaining such institutions throughout the variations of our economic fortunes, which are regarded as superficial phenomena. The principles of conservatism are traditional—the handing down from generation to generation of a cultural pattern, expressed in a form that is hieratic or aristocratic.

Reactionaryism is a negative doctrine. It vigorously denounces an existing situation—the situation as such—and seeks to establish a contrary situation. It is revolution in reverse. The contrary situation is not necessarily conservative or traditional—a reacting communist may seek to establish a totalitarian democracy completely at variance with the aristocratic principles of conservatism; and there is a wide choice of nihilistic attitudes, some of which we shall deal with. Nothing could be further from conservatism of the type given philosophical status by Bolingbroke and Burke than the fascist doctrines of Mussolini, Hitler and Franco, politicians who are to be regarded as reactionaries in our sense of the word, as counter-revolutionaries.

There is a further preliminary distinction to be made. Conscious of their regressive direction, reactionaries are always anxious to deny the existence of *progress*. This is an emotive word and must be handled with care. To deny progress of any kind is merely to be impervious to certain facts. The general standard of living, for example, is now higher in Britain and the United States than at any other period in history. This is proved by such statistics as the general expectancy of life, the infant mortality rate, the incidence of epidemic diseases and so on. That this material progress has been accompanied by minor set-backs must be admitted; and there has been no moral advance at all to correspond with this rise in the standard of living. We enjoy our modern comforts with uneasy consciences.

But we are not at present concerned with the standard of living, or any other form of material progress, but with the cultural phenomenon called art. In this sphere no responsible historian or philosopher would venture to claim anything in the nature of evolutionary progress. New materials and tools have from time to time been discovered and introduced, and these have led to a wider application of the aesthetic sensibility. But sensibility itself, both in its executive and appreciative aspects, is just as constant as any other human faculty, and certainly does not seem to have made any 'progress' or any regress in the past 400 centuries.

If there has been no progress or regress there has been constant *change*. The Stone Age, the Iron Age, the Bronze Age; the Classical Age, the Medieval Age, the Modern Age—these are vast cyclical changes in civilization and in all that is characteristic of a civilization—its art, religion and philosophy. Within these cyclical epochs are alternating phases that exhibit even more drastic contrasts—for example, within the Stone Age we pass from the naturalistic art of the palæolithic period to the abstract or geometrical art of the neolithic period. Similar alternations occur in all the Ages, and in our own age, we seem to be in the process of repeating the change from a naturalistic to a geometrical type of art. Such cyclical changes are always broken up into gradual but definite stages—the stages we recognize historically by labels such as Mannerist, Baroque, Rococo; Romantic, Classic; Realism, Impressionism, Post-Impressionism, Cubism, Superrealism and Constructivism.

Admittedly, the more minute we become in our historical analysis, the less universal are our categories. Romantic and Classic are styles that can be recognized throughout history—and they have definite correspondences in social structures and psychological types. By contrast a movement like Impressionism is to be explained by local and incidental factors that do not necessarily recur.

Change, however, is persistent enough, and it is difficult to see how it could be arrested, short of the death of mankind. Existence itself is a changeful process—a process of conception, gestation, birth, growth and decay. If we were dealing with animal life, we could contemplate an endless repetition of this cyclic process, until the species exhausted itself or was superseded by another species. But man is self-conscious and it is his peculiarity that he has gradually extended the range of his consciousness. This has been a very slow process, and again we must hesitate to use the word 'progress'. But the consciousness of, say, the Cavendish professor of physics, or the Astronomer Royal, or a mystic like Simone Weil, is infinitely more comprehensive than the consciousness of an Australian bushman. It is possible, of course, that the Australian bushman is conscious of one or two things that escape the Astronomer Royal; and it is doubtful if the consciousness of animal vitality possessed and expressed by the palæolithic artist has ever been subsequently exceeded. It would seem that one kind of consciousness supersedes other kinds: there is a certain balance of intensities—the sense of magic, the sense of mystery, the sense of glory: from time to time all these phases of consciousness have in some degree been sacrificed to allow a rational consciousness to develop. But it would be rather perverse to maintain that the consciousness of an Einstein represented no qualitative advance on the consciousness of a tribal witch-doctor.

I believe that aesthetic consciousness—the consciousness of formal beauty and organic vitality—is a basic consciousness, and that the witch-doctor and Einstein are equally dependent on it. Progress in human consciousness depends on this aesthetic faculty, but the faculty itself, as I have already suggested, shows no progress. It is the formative principle in human evolution, and it is what is formed that indicates progress, not any change in the instrument of formation. This may seem a fine distinction, but it is essential to an understanding of the history of art. It enables us to understand and appreciate what is basic in such diverse forms of art as Greek classicism, medieval sublimity, Renaissance humanism, nineteenth-century realism, and contemporary abstract art. There is a formative principle that is constant in all this diversity: but there are also successive changes of appearance to meet the spirit of each age.

The Spirit of the Age, the German *Zeitgeist*, is a dangerous phenomenon to flirt with, but it is doubtful if we can escape its wiles. There is always a conflict between the formative principle and the *Zeitgeist*: between the will to a form that is absolute and universal, and the will to a mode of expression that is immediately effective or acceptable. It is beyond our power to avoid this conflict, for the simple reason that we are most firmly in the grip of the *Zeitgeist* when we are least aware of its presence in our consciousness. Certainly we do not escape it by deliberately offering what we, in our near-sightedness, designate as *zeitgeistlich*: that is merely another attempt to lift ourselves up by our own bootstraps. Even the self-assured objectivity of the scholar may be the *Zeitgeist* in disguise: one thinks of all the dead learning embodied in seventeenth-century theology, or in nineteenth-century history!

I do not wish to identify the changeful process exhibited by history with the spirit of each successive age. Some changes are profound; others are superficial. The Romantic Movement in art and literature was a profound change, and has not yet exhausted itself: the Gothic Revival was a superficial change, the spirit of the age in fancy costume. The same distinction must be made between the changes we have witnessed in the twentieth century. The new conception of the physical structure of the universe is probably a change profound in itself, and with profound philosophical consequences. The question we have to ask ourselves, with the knowledge that we cannot answer it with any certainty, is whether the changes in art, which are just as astonishing, are equally profound.

The two changes—in science and in art—have been concurrent, and for this reason alone it is fair to assume that they are in some manner interrelated. The religious change known as the Reformation can be ascribed to many causes, such as the corruption of the clergy and the overweening economic power of the monasteries; but a new religious attitude (as opposed to a reactionary religious attitude) was made possible by a new theory of the universe, put forward by Galileo and Copernicus. The Reformation could have been a reaction (to a more primitive and 'purer' conception of Christianity); instead it was a change in religious sensibility corresponding to a change in scientific knowledge.

I believe that modern art has the same consequential character. It is a change in modes of perception and imagination that corresponds to a new spiritual or intellectual attitude widely shared by modern man. This is not a formal or conscious attitude: the artist is not 'expressing', as we say, a scientific or a philosophical view of the world in conformity with the latest views of the physicists or the metaphysicians, or of the politicians and economists. On such matters he may sincerely profess a profound ignorance. Nevertheless, there exists a widely diffused sentiment, a sense of bewilderment, of anxiety, to which all these specialists have contributed their share, and this atmosphere the artist, since he is by definition a being acutely sensitive to such collective intimations, cannot escape. He finds symbols to represent these prevalent states of human consciousness: that is his primary function in society.

We cannot tell whether he finds the right symbols, but the success of the contemporary artist is due to a general recognition that he has found such symbols, and has given them convincing form. The artists of our period thus made 'great' by our recognition of their symbolic potency—artists like Picasso, Klee, Kandinsky, Léger—are all artists who have proliferated new symbolic forms—forms that correspond in some intimate way to the *Zeitgeist*.

So much for the process of change. We see that it is inevitable, that there is nothing inherently good in it, that it represents no kind of progress, moral or aesthetic. But this process is not mechanical: it involves human beings, and most of all it involves the artist. I do not say that the artist is the agent of change;

indeed the perfect work of art lifts us out of the flux of existence, involves the observer in a state of timeless contemplation: but each moment of vision is a moment of arrest—it is not reached without movement.

The artist in such a situation 'lives on his nerves'. He is for ever analysing an unknown substance, attempting to resolve a mystery, to give form to vague intuitions. It is little wonder, therefore, that some artists break down under the strain. Some of those who cannot stand the pace simply fall back, abandon the effort; but there are others, and it is this particular type that I wish to isolate and examine, who stay to mock, to recriminate, to abuse, to betray. If the strain becomes unbearable to a whole generation, then we may get that historical phenomenon which Gilbert Murray, in a famous lecture on such a period in Greek history, called a 'failure of nerve'. He used this phrase to describe the inability of the ancient world to maintain the rational idealism of the great schools of the fourth century B.C.—the relapse into superstition, mysticism, gnosticism, revelation, out of which a new positive faith, primitive Christianity, eventually emerged. The present failure of nerve is not so predominantly superstitious, though we must remember that the Nazis had their Rosenberg, and nothing can be so ideologically irrational as the cults of race and power that characterize reactionary politics. Since we are dealing with art, which is a symbolic activity, we cannot properly speak of a failure to maintain a philosophy of rational idealism. But nevertheless, reason is involved in the present situation, and it is not found on the side of reaction.

Here I must stress a distinction that I have been making all my life between reason and scientific method. But let me on this occasion rely on Gilbert Murray, whose name I have just evoked. At the end of the essay in question he has an eloquent passage which I would like to quote:

'The Uncharted surrounds us on every side and we must needs have some relation towards it, a relation which will depend on the general discipline of a man's mind and the bias of his whole character. As far as knowledge and conscious reason will go, we should follow resolutely their austere guidance. When they cease, as cease they must, we must use as best we can those fainter powers of apprehension and surmise and sensitiveness by which, after all, most high truth has been reached as well as most high art and poetry; careful always really to seek for truth and not for our own emotional satisfaction, careful not to neglect the real needs of men and women through basing our life on dreams; and remembering above all to walk gently in a world where the lights are dim and the very stars wander.'[1]

Here is an admission, by an apostle of reason, that knowledge and *conscious* reason will only carry us so far in an understanding of reality, and that when we reach the limit of their powers, 'we must use as best we can those fainter powers of apprehension and surmise and sensitiveness by which, after all, most high truth has been reached as well as most high art and poetry'. I believe that Professor Murray puts these processes in their wrong order—that it is only when we have first used these powers of apprehension and surmise and sensitiveness that it becomes possible to use the powers of conscious reason, for reason is not a wholly conceptual activity, a spinning of abstraction from mental vacuity: it is, in so far as it remains vital, a metaphorical activity, given energy and scope by the imagination. In other words, reason is fed, as from an underground source, by metaphors and symbols grasped in their sensuous actuality by a sensitive organism. It is better, therefore, to regard reason as inclusive of symbolic discourse; but at the same time to distinguish it

---

[1] *Five Stages of Greek Religion.* London (Watts), 1953, p. 171.

sharply from revelation and other supernatural modes of knowledge.

That contemporary art has its hermetic schools is not to be denied: some of the more pretentious adepts of superrealism were as irrational as the Gnostics or Mithras-worshippers described by Professor Murray. But in general, modern art, in spite of its strangeness and obscurity, has been inspired by a rational desire to chart the Uncharted. If in such an attempt it has produced symbols that are unfamiliar, that was only to be expected, for the depths it has been exploring are mysterious depths, full of strange fish. Some of these might perhaps have been left at the bottom of the sea—they are monsters that evolution has discarded. But if we persist in our restless desire to know everything about the universe and ourselves, then we must not be afraid of what the artist brings back from his voyage of discovery.

I am not thinking only of the so-called dream-images, of the symbols of the unconscious, of all the misshapen progeny of frustration and inhibition. The artists' images are above all formative—that is to say, they give defined shape to what was amorphous; they are crystallizations of fluid mental intuitions; they materialize the immaterial, the immature, the merely sensed and located directions of significant experience. What is best in so-called abstract art—which is not 'abstract', but actually a concretion of what was suspended in abstraction—belongs to this kind of imaginative activity. It is frontier work in the process of reasoning: the invention of the necessary symbols for an advance of consciousness.

It is this kind of work that has been branded as 'extremism'. The label is not a dishonourable one, for all pioneers in human endeavour have been extremists, explorers working at the frontiers of experience—if they are artists, working at the frontiers of perceptual experience. To refuse to work in such an arduous climate is understandable: in any case it is a task for the chosen few only, for those endowed by nature with the necessary sensitiveness and courage. But what I wish to discuss now is the case of the pioneer who deserts this front, who retires to a safe distance from which he can revile his former collaborators.

Of course, such an artist never was a whole-hearted collaborator. The renegade type is a born schizoid, suspicious of his fellows from the moment he recognizes that he has fellows— that is to say, sibling rivals to a mother's affection. When we come across the envious and resentful artist, it is always legitimate to suspect an irregular or disorganized childhood—a lack of mother-love in early infancy, divorced or separated parents, a social environment of insecurity and anxiety. It is difficult and perhaps dangerous to probe into the case-histories of our contemporary renegades: but nothing that we know about the early history of typical specimens would seem to contradict this hypothesis. Fortunately we can find our evidence in the past.

Wordsworth is a typical case of the pathological renegade. That he was 'neurotic' is not a new diagnosis—Matthew Arnold and J. K. Stephen already recognized this fact, though they did not have our modern clinical phraseology. It has been left to Mr. F. W. Bateson to describe the pattern of this psychosis, and to trace its origins back to an unhappy childhood, where all conflicts of this type originate.[2] The great poetry of Wordsworth was the product of a single decade, and according to Mr. Bateson— and may I say I entirely agree with him on this significant point—was generated by a struggle for normality and mental health. 'So far from surrendering to the neurotic elements in his personality,' writes Mr. Bateson, 'as so many Romantic poets have done, Wordsworth's early life was one long desperate struggle against them. And whatever one's reservations about this or that poem the general direction of the poetry is undoubtedly towards sanity, sincerity, sympathy, gaiety—in a word, the

[2] *Wordsworth: a Re-interpretation.* London (Longmans), 1951.

humane virtues. What makes their successful realization in Wordsworth's best poems so exhilarating to the modern reader is his continuous consciousness of how hardly the successes have been won, how precarious the achievement is. There were no easy victories for him either as a man or a poet.'

The word schizoid means 'divided'—a divided personality is the layman's term for this psychological condition. In J. K. Stephen's cruel verses[3] the two parts of Wordsworth's divided personality are called 'The Two Voices':

> There are two Voices: one is of the deep;
> It learns the storm-cloud's thundrous melody,
> Now roars, now murmurs with the changing sea,
> Now bird-like pipes, now closes soft in sleep.
> And one is of an old half-witted sheep
> Which bleats articulate monotony,
> And indicates that two and one are three,
> The grass is green, lakes damp, and mountains steep
> And, Wordsworth, both are thine . . .

This is an acute analysis in so far as it recognizes that one voice is of the deep—that is to say, comes from the unconscious; and the other is objective, directed to the outer world. The normal person stills the voice of the deep, orientates himself to the outer world, becomes a good mixer, a conservative in politics and a reactionary in art. The psychotic person surrenders to his subjective self, shuns society, is suspicious of his fellow-workers, is sexually morbid and philosophically pessimistic or nihilistic. But a few rare people are conscious of both tendencies within the self, and can hold them in a precarious balance. It is a view I have long held that most great art and literature proceeds from this

---

[3] Originally, Mr. Bateson tells us, contributed to the University magazine *Granta* in June, 1891.

condition of precarious mental equilibrium—the great artist is 'a tight-rope walker'.[4]

Mr. Bateson seems to admit this fact in the case of Wordsworth; but he also agrees that the achievement of normality, the triumph of The Second Voice, meant an end to the writing of any vital poetry. But he might have extended his analysis to show that the same triumph of the Second Voice meant an end to his friendship with Coleridge, a grudging envy of rival poets like Byron and Shelley, a vicious and ruthless reactionaryism in politics, and a hardening of the heart which made of him an old man unloved by his neighbours and little respected by his younger contemporaries.

In his early manhood Wordsworth had been a revolutionary in politics and an experimentalist in poetics. He and Coleridge together created a new type of poetry, the poetry of sincerity, what Keats called 'the true voice of feeling'. Wordsworth did not welcome this quality in the younger generation. Keats he thought 'over-luscious'; the 'Ode on a Grecian Urn' only served to remind him of one of his own inferior sonnets, and the 'Hymn to Pan' he characterized as 'a pretty piece of paganism'. But it is his attitude towards Goethe that is most significant, for Goethe is the typical poet of equilibrium, a writer who can balance his senses against his intellect, and from their tension project throughout his life the highest poetry. But for Wordsworth there was in all this 'a profligacy, an inhuman sensuality ... which is utterly revolting'.[5] For Wordsworth Goethe is a 'poetical sensualist'—'He had not sufficiently clear moral perceptions to make him anything but an artificial writer.'[6]

---

[4] G. Melchiori has given us a brilliant survey of modern poetry from this point of view. Cf. The Tightrope Walkers, London (Routledge & Kegan Paul), 1956.

[5] Bishop Christopher Wordsworth's reminiscences of 1827, Memoirs, ii, 478.

[6] Lady Richardson, August 26, 1841; Grosart III, 435–6. Wordsworth's reaction to 'sensualism' is another matter, which I have dealt with in my book on Wordsworth and which Mr. Bateson also analyses.

'Of Goethe Wordsworth spoke with his usual bitterness', says Crabb Robinson in one of the entries in his *Diary* (1 January, 1843), and this 'usual bitterness' was reserved for a contemporary poet of universal fame who had dared to be personal—to make his emotions and experiences the deliberate basis of his work. Wordsworth had dared do that for a decade only, between the years 1797 and 1808. Then he clamped down his senses, shut out his emotions and became what he accuses Goethe of being—'a very artificial writer'. But artificiality has a special meaning for Wordsworth: he defines it as 'aiming to be universal, and yet constantly exposing his individuality, which his character was not of a kind to dignify'.[7]

Here we have a distinction between individuality and character which I have also discussed elsewhere, maintaining precisely the opposite of Wordsworth's opinion—namely, that all true poetry proceeds from the personality or individuality of man, and that character is the social trap in which the poet is caught and extinguished. However, that distinction is not in question now, except in so far as the reactionary in our own time adopts a moral tone, condemning extremities in art as a danger to the State, or as the corruption of society, etc. It is not often that such critics have a moral habit to match their moral sentiments; morality is merely one more stick in their armoury of resentment.

I want now to turn from the real case of Wordsworth to the imaginary case of a modern painter who has this schizoid temperament, who in early infancy has acquired, through neglect or lack of maternal sympathy, intense feelings of unfulfilled desire. As the child grows up and adapts himself to the outer world, these feelings are suppressed and by a process now clearly understood by psychology, they become death wishes directed against other people, instincts of hatred and aggression. All that

[7] Ibid.

infantile distress is now blamed on someone else, it may be on the ruling classes, or the Jews, or some foreign nation. But we are considering the imaginary case of a painter who is thus afflicted—a painter, moreover, who early exhibits signs of genius. It is impossible to nurse in that same breast instincts of hatred and aggression that are *destructive* and instincts of love and sympathy that are *creative*. The destructive instincts will gradually overcome the creative instincts, the point of equilibrium will be passed, and the painter's talent will as a consequence gradually decline.

As soon as he becomes aware of this process—sees his own creative powers declining at the same time as the powers of other contemporary artists increase in strength and beauty he will be *consumed* (as we rightly say) with envy. He will project the destructive forces raging in his own psyche on to these success-ful contemporaries, and they and their friends will become ver-itable *demons*, forces working for the destruction of art itself. Such an artist may go so far as to disown art: he will cease to practise painting and remain a remote and disdainful spectator. Some of the Dadaists were of this type. But more often such an artist becomes a renegade, a reactionary, and turns to attack those whose aspirations he once shared. It did not need modern psychology to detect this form of reaction—Aesop described it in the fable of the fox and the grapes.

At this point I would like to quote a passage from Joan Rivi-ere's essay on 'Hate, Greed and Aggression'[8]—a beautifully clear summary of this aspect of emotional life:

> Turning away in contempt or rejection from a desired object can be a dangerous psychological reaction, if it is not used merely as a restraint on greed, and especially if revenge and

[8] *Love, Hate and Reparation*. Two lectures by Melanie Klein and Joan Riviere. Hogarth Press and The Inst. of Psychoanalysis, London, 1937.

retaliation inspire it as well. The most impressive evidence of this may be seen when such a reaction leads to suicide—when disappointment and the fury of revenge engender such hatred and contempt of life and all it offers that life itself is finally rejected and destroyed.

The revengeful wish to disappoint, leading on to the reaction of contempt, is one main source of all the countless varieties of faithlessness, betrayal, desertion, infidelity and treachery so constantly manifested in life, particularly by special types of people in whom this mechanism is strongly pronounced— from the Don Juans or the prostitutes (in sexual matters) to the rolling stones who never keep to one job or one line of work (in self-preservative matters). Such people spend their lives seeking, then finding, then being disappointed because their desires are inordinate and unrealizable either in quality or degree; ultimately they turn away, spurn and reject—only to start the search instantly all over again.

We can easily think of a type of contemporary artist who perfectly illustrates this psychological 'reaction of contempt', who betrays the principles he once served, and turns in revengeful spite on artists with whom he once shared a dangerous enterprise. But do not let us return contempt for contempt, or revenge for revenge. We do not envy such people, so why should we do more than try to understand them and if possible forgive them. They would welcome retaliation, of course, for that would satisfy their instinct for self-destruction; 'indirect enjoyment they get in feeling deprived and injured by others.'[9] I think that the only right attitude (apart from a clinical one, which we must leave to the psychiatrist) is to treat such people with understanding, which implies tolerance and even sympathy. Any direct reasoning with an unbalanced mind of this kind is quite useless: it

[9] Joan Riviere, p. 30.

would only inspire further abuse, further sadistic fantasies. Moreover, a return to reason in such cases is not to be expected, so persistent is the drive to self-destruction.

To adopt an attitude of tolerance in such a situation may seem to be self-righteous, but I have no wish to claim infallibility, either for this analysis of reactionaryism in the arts, or for tolerance itself, which is sometimes a cover for lack of judgement. 'To be guided by one's aversions,' writes Gilbert Murray in the essay from which I have already quoted, 'is always a sign of weakness or defeat.' I think that exactly describes the weakness or defeat of the type of disappointed artist we have been considering. But Professor Murray continues—'it is as much a failure of nerve to reject blindly for fear of being a fool, as to believe blindly for fear of missing some emotional stimulus'. Perhaps some of us have been guilty of believing blindly in certain phases of modern art, and we may have been emotionally deceived. But 'to reject blindly for fear of being a fool', or in order to assuage the feelings of hatred and destructiveness within oneself—that seems to me to be the greater weakness, the more overwhelming defeat. A failure of nerve is a betrayal of human endeavour in its deepest commitment—in the search for reality, for the 'most high truth'. Modern art has conducted such a search, and the best of modern artists, among whom I have no hesitation in including certain abstract painters and sculptors, as well as corresponding poets, musicians and architects, have been and still are engaged in a spiritual enterprise which may one day be reckoned as a decisive phase in the history of human culture.

We are all too deeply involved in this enterprise, either as pioneers and partisans, or as renegades and apostates, to affect, with any absolute right, judicial detachment. Who is not with the historical present is against it: we can analyse scientifically only the dead body of the past. It may be argued that the wise man will avoid any position of extremism; but wisdom in that case is merely another name for caution. What has been worth while in human history—the great achievements of physics and astronomy, of geographical discovery and of human healing, of philosophy and of art—has been the work of extremists—of those who have believed in the absurd, dared the impossible, and in the face of all reaction and denial, have cried *Eppur si muove!*

12

THE PROBLEM OF PORNOGRAPHY

I propose to limit my considerations of this difficult subject to the discussion of the following four propositions:

(1) Pornography is a social problem: it is a commodity brought into existence by certain characteristics of a highly developed civilization.
(2) The problem cannot be solved by any form of prohibition or censorship. These forcible methods merely aggravate the disease, and there are other deplorable consequences.
(3) Prevention is better than cure. By diagnosing the psychological motives of those who produce and those who consume pornography, we may be able to sublimate the instincts involved.
(4) Any form of censorship, political or moral, inhibits the development of spiritual values. Morality itself is strengthened by liberty.

I

In recent public discussions of the subject, of which the legal proceedings against *Lady Chatterley's Lover* are typical, pornography has been considered almost exclusively as a form of literature, and the etymology of the word certainly justifies such a limitation of its meaning. It is perhaps worth emphasizing, however, that -graphy is an ambiguous suffix, and in such words as lithography and photography suggests a picture rather than the written word. In journalism a graphic description is one that conveys information chiefly by the use of images and metaphors.

And so in pornography there is a 'filthy picture', either directly presented, or evoked by words. An enormous amount of art and literature is erotic in the sense that it stimulates vague sexual emotions, but it has no pornographic intention or effect because 'it leaves everything to the imagination'. The consumer has to invent his own images, and it is felt, I do not know with what justification, that there is no harm in this. In any case, the liberty of the private imagination cannot be restricted by any public means, though perhaps Plato and Pavlov (and George Orwell satirically) played with the possibility.

In pornography a visual or verbal image acts as a direct stimulus to the erotic drives or impulses which are always latent and ready to be stimulated in normal people. There are pornographic images that are too crude or too obscure to have the required effect: they are just bad of their kind. 'Good' pornography implies adequate artistic skill, and this skill may be so great that it provokes the well-known argument of artistic justification. I myself have used this argument in the past, but I do not now think that it is a very logical one. Indeed, there is cogent reason for the view that the more artistic the images are made, the more effective they will be, and therefore the more reprehensible from the ethical and legal point of view. As a matter of fact, very few great artists have carried on any deliberate pornographic activity. The pornographic incidents which can be culled from Chaucer or Shakespeare are part of the realistic integrity of these writers. But 'realistic integrity' is a cant phrase that might be used to excuse Rabelais or Casanova, as it has been used to excuse D. H. Lawrence. It is better, therefore, to get down to the psychological roots of the problem before attempting such arbitrary distinctions.

The infant, according to Freud, is a raging lustful sexual maniac almost from the moment of birth, and the large amount of child analysis that has been done since Freud's time has fully confirmed this diagnosis. But the child's aggressive sexuality is suppressed in the first four years of its weaning and social adaptation, and it then enters into a 'latency period' (roughly from six or seven to fourteen years) during which it presents to the world that conventional symbol of innocency which is the opposite of pornography. Then, from about fourteen years onwards, conscious sexual desires are reanimated and a censorship, hitherto unconscious, becomes active and is associated with various external authorities, parental or social. The sexual images that had rioted freely in infancy are revived in an atmosphere of moral restraint. Feelings of guilt supervene and free indulgence not only in sexual acts but even in sexual fantasies become a sin or even a crime.

A certain measure of moral restraint is accepted by most people as the price that must be paid for civilization: mutual understanding, mutual aid, altruism in general becomes the rule, and as such represents the triumph of the ego-ideal over our selfish instincts. But this ideal is a precarious achievement, and in many cases, and for many different reasons, may break down. What usually happens then is that conflicts which have been experienced in infancy and afterwards forgotten are revived in the unconscious and provide the stimulus or driving force for sexual fantasies.

Memory, as the Greeks already recognized, is the mother of

art and poetry, and Ernest Schachtel, in a famous and fascinating paper,[1] has shown how works of art may be interpreted as efforts to penetrate the screen of verbal clichés which a civilization elaborates to keep infantile experiences hidden. A society cannot allow the recovery of these experiences because the very memory of them would shatter the conventions upon which civilization depends to its continuance. At this point I would like to quote a key passage from Schachtel's essay:

'No doubt the hostility of Western civilization to pleasure, and to sexual pleasure as the strongest of all, is a most important factor operative in the transformation and education of the child into an adult who will be able to fulfil the role and the functions he has to take over in society and will be satisfied by them. Freud has not only called attention to the phenomenon of childhood amnesia but has also singled out a decisive factor in its genesis. I believe, however, that two points are important for a more adequate understanding of the phenomenon. First, it is not sufficiently clear why a repression of sexual experience should lead to a repression of all experience in early childhood. For this reason the assumption seems more likely that there must be something in the general quality of childhood experience which leads to the forgetting of that experience. Second, the phenomenon of childhood amnesia leads to a problem regarding the nature of repression, especially repression of childhood material. The term and concept of repression suggest that material which *per se* could be recalled is excluded from recall because of its traumatic nature. If the traumatic factor can be clarified and dissolved, the material is again accessible to recall. But even the most profound and prolonged psychoanalysis does not lead to a recovery of childhood

[1] Originally published in *Psychiatry*, 1947 (Vol. 10, pp. 1–26). More accessible in *An Outline of Psychoanalysis*, ed. Clara Thompson and others. The Modern Library (New York), 1955, pp. 203–26.

memory; at best it unearths some incidents and feelings that had been forgotten. Childhood amnesia, then, may be due to a formation of the memory functions which makes them unsuitable to accommodate childhood experience, rather than exclusively to a censor repressing objectionable material which, without such repression, could and would be remembered. The adult is usually not capable of experiencing what the child experiences; more often than not he is not even capable of imagining what the child experiences. It would not be surprising, then, that he should be incapable of recalling his own childhood experiences since his whole mode of experiencing has changed. The person who remembers is the present person, a person who has changed considerably, whose interests, needs, fears, capacity for experience and emotion have changed. The two mechanisms of forgetting suggested here shade gradually and imperceptibly into one another. They are neither alternatives nor opposites, but rather the two ends of a continuous scale.'[2]

If to this description of childhood amnesia we add the horrifying descriptions of infantile sexual aggressiveness revealed in the analysis of children by Melanie Klein, Anna Freud, Therese Benedek and others, we can get some conception of the dangers that accompany any attempt to tap these buried memories. If the controls are adequate the suppressed images can be released with just sufficient force to give an impetus to our fantasies and vitality to the words and images in which imagination finds expression. It is as if dullness or stupefaction were the general condition of a mind that can from time to time be brought to life by a whiff from a cylinder of compressed oxygen. More than a whiff is too much of a good thing and produces some form of paranoia—that is to say, a flow of imagery that cannot be

---

[2] Ibid., pp. 208–9.

accommodated to normal (civilized) experience. Pornography is an excess of this kind.

If, as I believe, Schachtel's theory is sound and cultures therefore 'vary in the degree to which they impose clichés on experience and memory', then 'the more a society develops in the direction of mass conformism, whether such development be achieved by a totalitarian pattern or within a democratic framework by means of the employment market, education, the patterns of social life, advertising, Press, radio, movies, best-sellers, and so on, the more stringent becomes the rule of the conventional experience and memory *schemata* in the lives of the members of that society'. Of such memory *schemata*, the myth of happy and innocent childhood is the most prevalent and powerful because, as Schachtel points out, 'it bolsters parental authority and maintains a conventional prop of the authority of the family by asserting that one's parents were good and benevolent people who did everything for the good of their children, however much they may have done against it'. But the purpose of the myth is to disguise the fact that early childhood was not a period of happiness, but one in which the child abandoned himself completely to pleasure and satisfaction, and thus came into conflict with parental authority and social conventions. In later life the memory of this conflict is not altogether suppressed—it is screened. Indeed, as Schachtel points out, one can distinguish two processes which overlap and shade into each other. 'One process leaves the culturally unacceptable or unusable experiences and the memory thereof to starvation by the expedient of providing no linguistic, conceptual and memory *schemata* for them and by channelling later experience into the experience *schemata* of the culture. . . . Compared with this process, the dynamism of the taboo and of repression of individually or culturally tabooed experience and strivings is like the nightstick of the policeman compared with the gradual, slow, insinuating process of education in which some things are just not mentioned and others said to be for the best of the child.'

The subtlety of the process of forgetting, which Schachtel analyses so carefully, does not really concern us now. Whether bludgeoned into insensibility by taboos and laws, or insensibly educated into blissful forgetfulness, the effect is the same. Sex becomes a dirty word and all publication and celebration of sexual insubordination becomes that disreputable phenomenon we are discussing—pornography.

To understand is to forgive, even in this sphere. But the problem exists and most people would admit that it is better for all of us to believe in the myth of a happy childhood than to revive the reality of the sexual conflicts of childhood. But I think some of us would maintain that the process of adjustment could be made with more understanding and with less violence to memory and imagination. Repression is one process, but sublimation is another. 'Pseudo-experience in terms of conventional clichés' is one way of adaptation to society; the transformation of revived memory into myth and aesthetic reality is another way of adaptation, but not one which is *deliberately* adopted by any civilized society in the modern world.

I have suggested that pornography is a characteristic of highly developed civilizations—it might have been more correct to say of decadent civilizations. But we all have our different conceptions of maturity and decadence, and mine does not necessarily imply the high intellectual attainments of a period like the fifth century in Athens or the seventeenth century in Europe. There are many so-called primitive societies (the Balinese before the Europeans arrived) where sexual experience is transformed into drama or dance and where pornography is unknown. Pornography, though it existed, was not a problem in Athens—drama was the transforming *schema* for the infantile conflicts (for which good reason we now speak of the Oedipus complex). In general, however, we must not look for ideal solutions in the past. Though the great poets have instinctively understood the problem and solved it in their mythologies, it is only now, when we begin to understand the processes of memory and amnesia *scientifically*, that a social solution of the problem is conceivable.

I am not going to be so pretentious as to indicate the programme for such a solution. It involves a complete reorientation of our educational methods and ideals (I have given a general sketch of such methods in *Education Through Art*). But, briefly, pornography would become otiose if the situation that creates the need for it did not exist—if, that is to say, the Oedipal situation could be transformed, but realistically transformed. The only kind of transformation that is realistic is the transformation accomplished by the aesthetic experience. The distinction between art and illusion is a distinction between a lost experience that has been recovered and made a part of the present reality, and a lost experience that remains unconscious because it is screened in clichés and ready-made conventions of morality. Someone has said that art is the invention of new clichés. It would be more to the point to define true education as the prevention of cliché formation—which is what I mean by education through art. To quote Schachtel for the last time (it is the conclusion of his essay): 'Memory cannot be entirely extinguished in man, his capacity for experience cannot be entirely suppressed by schematization. It is in those experiences which transcend the cultural *schemata*, in those memories of experience which transcend the conventional memory *schemata*, that every new insight and every true work of art have their origin, and that the hope of progress, of a widening of the scope of human endeavour and human life, is founded.'

II

Taboo is a comparatively gentle method of attempting to control the vicious sexual fantasies of a civilized society;

prohibition and censorship are brutal methods which succeed only in aggravating the disease. Although everyone is tired of *Lady Chatterley's Lover*, I shall try to prove this point by a close look at D. H. Lawrence, and I shall begin with a personal reminiscence.

In the autumn of 1915 I was a young subaltern in a camp on Cannock Chase waiting to be drafted to the Front. I had already become acquainted with Lawrence's work through the short stories that had appeared in the *English Review* and I had read *The White Peacock* (1911), *The Trespasser* (1912) and *Sons and Lovers* (1913) with growing enthusiasm. In order to make sure that I got a copy of *The Rainbow* which had been announced in the summer of 1915, I placed a direct order with the publisher, Methuen, and it reached me on the day of publication, 30 September. I read the book with enthusiasm and without the slightest sense of offence. About five weeks later, a few days before I left for the Front, I heard that it had been seized by the police and all further sales suppressed. I remember the anger I felt at the time and that I wrote an impulsive letter of sympathy to the author.

I mention this personal experience because my admiration for Lawrence at that time was pure and disinterested, and it was the action of the police that first suggested to me that a writer of obvious sincerity and high moral purpose could be regarded as obscene or pornographic and prosecuted in a public court. My disbelief in censorship is based on the sense of injustice I then felt. Further, I do not believe that up to that time (I was then twenty-one) I had been aware of pornography as such. Police action put the idea into my head.

The effect on Lawrence himself was disastrous. At first he reacted calmly enough, but it was a turning-point in his life. From that moment he was convinced that England was finished, and he 'struggled like a fly on a treacle paper' to leave the country. 'As for the novel', he wrote to Edward Marsh, about the suppression of *The Rainbow*, 'I am not surprised. Only the most horrible feeling of hopelessness has come over me lately—I feel as if the whole thing were coming to an end—the whole of England, of the Christian era: as if ours was the age only of Decline and Fall. It almost makes one die. I cannot bear it—this England, this past.'

More inwardly he was hurt to the quick of his soul. He felt as if the very springs of creation had been blocked by ignorant but powerful forces. He had written *The Rainbow* with great conviction—'it is a big book,' he told Edward Marsh, 'and one of the important novels in the language. I tell you, who know.' But how could he go on writing with this threat of suppression continually before him? Such an inhibition cannot be tolerated by any creative artist.

From that moment I believe he resolved to hurl such defiance at 'the grey ones of the world' that the concept of pornography would become meaningless. For Lawrence had come to the conclusion that pornography was a question of secrecy. 'Without secrecy there would be no pornography.' Pornography is a sign of a diseased condition of the body politic and 'the way to treat the disease is to come out into the open with sex and sex stimulus'. A smug and corrupt society had challenged a creative artist of passionate purity of intention and high moral courage. Lawrence accepted the challenge and the rest of his creative life was a martyrdom in this cause.

For the moment I am not concerned with the rightness of Lawrence's remedy, but with making the point that suppression of *The Rainbow* was the immediate cause of a reaction that eventually led to the writing and publication of *Lady Chatterley's Lover*. The censors, acting on behalf of 'the ordinary vulgar people' with their 'dirty little secret', in November 1915 set up a whole chain of reactions that ended with the open sale of millions of copies of that book, and for ever exposed that 'dirty little secret' to the wholesome light.

But is that really the end of the matter? Is Lawrence right in assuming that 'to come out into the open with sex and sex stimulus' will cure the diseased condition of the body politic of which pornography is the symptom?

Lawrence himself did not really believe that the cure was as simple as that. He knew, better than most people, that the problem was one of social consciousness, or perhaps of social unconsciousness, and that a true condition of social consciousness can only be brought about by processes that involve the whole concept of 'normality'. We are governed, especially in the mass, by the vicious drives of an unconscious such as Freud postulated. The masses, in matters of sex, are more neurotic than the individual, and their neuroticism (their compulsive conformity) takes the form of an unyielding morality against which the sensitive individual rebels; his rebellion is his neuroticism. Social insanity breeds personal insanity, in endless circles of involvement.

Two forms of consciousness, therefore—human consciousness and social consciousness, in eternal conflict. These forms of consciousness must become aware of each other, must become *related*. And then the true self will be revealed. But today we are slaves to social consciousness. 'Sex does not exist; there is only sexuality. And sexuality is merely a greedy, blind self-seeking. Self-seeking is the real motive of sexuality. And therefore, since the thing sought is the same, the self, the mode of seeking is not very important. Heterosexual, homosexual, narcissistic, normal, or incest, it is all the same thing. It is just sexuality, not sex. It is one of the universal forms of self-seeking. Every man, every woman, just seeks his own self, her own self, in the sexual experience. It is the picture over again, whether in sexuality or self-sacrifice, greed or charity, the same thing, the self, the image, the idol, the image of me, and norm!

'The true self is not aware that it is a self. A bird, as it sings,

sings itself. But not according to a picture. It has no idea of itself.'[3]

In all considerations of this problem of pornography we must first get rid of the idea that it is a personal problem only—'the inadequacy', as Trigant Burrow calls it, 'of the view which posits a sick individual as over against a well society.' Pornography, like delinquency in general, is a social problem and it can only be solved by methods that involve social psychology—group analysis and group therapy. Of this truth psychoanalysts, from Freud to Burrow and Klein, have provided irrefutable evidence. The cure, if there is to be a cure, will involve every normal social activity from breast-feeding to the moral and political structure of the state. It means a complete reorientation of the aims and methods of education. Attempts to deal with the problem in any more isolated fashion are either ignorant or hypocritical.

III

We must approach any discussion of the process of sublimation very tentatively because it does not seem to me that psycho-analysts, or experts in the psychology of education, speak with any clear or united voice on the matter. Sublimation may be defined as 'the process of diverting unacceptable, unconscious libidinal drives into socially acceptable channels', a definition wide enough to cover every form of altruistic activity from scouting to sculpture, from nursing to scientific research. But in the limited sense in which I am going to discuss it briefly in the present context, sublimation means the transformation of libidinal drives (sexual instincts) into socially acceptable fantasies and symbols. Freud himself regarded the process as one of limited application and doubtful efficacy, but this was perhaps due to his

---

[3] From a review of Trigant Burrow's *The Social Basis of Consciousness*, 1927. *Phoenix* (1936) pp. 38, 1–2.

belief that the artist's gifts are fundamentally neurotic—'the art-ist', he wrote, 'has also an introverted disposition and has not far to go to become neurotic.[4] It would be difficult to prove that the average artist is any more neurotic than the average Philistine. Freud further believed that the artist is 'endowed with a powerful capacity for sublimation and with a certain flexibility in the repressions determining the conflict' (the conflict which might otherwise lead to a neurosis). The word 'endowed' seems to imply a faculty psychology not very characteristic of Freud's thought in general. A capacity for sublimation and a flexibility for repression are surely processes subject to variation and control, to training and education. And further, when Freud says that 'A true artist has more (than those who are not artists) at his dis-posal' in this process of sublimation because 'first of all he understands how to elaborate his day-dreams, so that they lose that personal note which grates upon strange ears and become enjoyable to others; he knows how to modify them sufficiently so that their origin in prohibited sources is not easily detected. Further, he possesses the mysterious ability to mould his particu-lar material until it expresses the ideas of his fantasy faithfully'— in all such statements he is ascribing to the artist unusual powers and mysterious abilities which do not really differ except in degree from the powers and abilities possessed at birth by every individual. I am not asserting that exceptional artists do not possess exceptional gifts of a psychosomatic origin, but what I do assert on the basis of a wide experience of artistic activities in young children is that all human beings are born with the cap-acity to elaborate their day-dreams, to mould their particular material until it expresses their fantasies faithfully. Every child is a potential artist in this sense, but education is at present con-ceived, not as a process of elaborating day-dreams, but as a

---

[4] This, and the succeeding quotations, come from *Introductory Lectures on Psychoanalysis*. Trans. Joan Riviere. London, 1922, pp. 314–15.

process of eliminating them altogether from the child's mental and practical life, and replacing them by social conventions and clichés of expression ('common sense') that drive the instincts underground, from where they emerge eventually in various forms of social aggressiveness, including pornography.

Pornography, therefore, is one more product of the rational tradition, of that process in history which Blake called 'an abstract objecting power that negatives everything:

'This is the Spectre of Man, the Holy Reasoning Power,
And in its Holiness is closed the Abomination of Desolation.'

That was, of course, also Lawrence's conclusion, and if the millions of people who read *Lady Chatterley's Lover* would only read his *Psychoanalysis and the Unconscious* (1921) and his *Fantasia of the Unconscious* (1927) there might be some hope of a change of mind and heart that would lead eventually to a new way of education, a new structure of society, and an end to sexual perversion and pornography, to mental illness of every kind, including juvenile delinquency and aggression.

The trouble with sex, Lawrence used to say, is that it has gone to the head. It has become an affair of instruction and understanding: it must be restored to the unconscious. 'Yet we *must* know, if only in order to learn not to know. The supreme lesson of human consciousness is to learn how *not to know*. That is, how not to *interfere* . . .

'Education means leading out the individual nature in each man and woman to its true fullness. You can't do that by stimulating the mind. To pump education into the mind is fatal. That which sublimates from the dynamic consciousness into the mental consciousness has alone any value. This, in most individuals, is very little indeed. So that most individuals, under a wise government, would be most carefully protected from all vicious attempts to inject extraneous ideas into them. Every extraneous idea, which has no inherent root in the dynamic consciousness, is as dangerous as a nail driven into a young tree. For the mass of people, knowledge must be symbolical, mythical, dynamic.'[5] Lawrence did not go on to say the 'higher, responsible, conscious class' who are able to create and interpret such symbols are the artists; and I think he was wrong to think of higher and lower classes in this connection. True symbols are not formed by classes or by individuals; they are archetypal, and proceed from the collective unconscious, as Jung has shown. Artists—seers of all kinds—are those who are capable of mediating—of acting as a bridge—between the group and the collective unconscious. Not leaders, as Lawrence dangerously called for, but mediators.

I shall proceed to argue in the next section that symbolization or sublimation is not enough: at any rate, it does not constitute the complete revolution in our attitude to sex that we need before the sexual instincts can 'come out into the open'. Sublimation of the sex instincts is the best we can do in the kind of society that is acceptable in the present stage of social evolution. It is more than a camouflage—it is a transformation. But by its very nature it cannot be 'understood'—the acceptance of it depends on its unconsciousness, on the fact that we do not really know what is taking place. But the real need, as Lawrence said, is consciousness—not self-consciousness (which we have) nor social consciousness (which we have lost), but relatedness, mutual consciousness, or dialogic consciousness as Martin Buber would call it. This is something that is not consistent with conventional morality: indeed, it requires the raising of conventional morality on to a spiritual level of which perhaps only Nietzsche has had any adequate conception—beyond Good and Evil.

[5] *Fantasia of the Unconscious* (1930 edn) pp. 67–8.

IV

My final argument is limited to the creative process itself, the mediative process, as we should more properly call it. It follows from what I have said (or what I have quoted Freud or Lawrence as saying) that the creation of a world of fantasy that mediates between our instincts and the society in which we live is an infinitely delicate process. Any false step in the direction of definite ideas, conceptualization, mental consciousness, will destroy the necessary spontaneity of the process. I believe that all who have given any deep thought to the nature of the creative or mediative activity we call art—Plato, Aristotle, Goethe, Schiller, Coleridge, Keats, Fiedler and Buber, to mention only the most perceptive—have agreed that spontaneity, unconsciousness, is the essential condition. 'The most superb mystery we have hardly recognized,' Lawrence called it: 'The immediate, instant self.' 'The fruitful zero,' Buber calls it; 'the headlong powers of utter newness'—an instinct of origination that is autonomous and not derivatory.

Modern psychologists are inclined to derive the multiform human soul from a single primal element—the 'libido', the 'will to power', and the like. But this is really only the generalization of certain degenerate states in which a single instinct not merely dominates but also spreads parasitically through the other. They begin with the cases (in our time of loss of community and oppression, the innumerable cases) where such a hypertrophy breeds the appearance of exclusiveness, they abstract rules from them, and apply them with the whole theoretical and practical questionableness of such applications. In opposition to these doctrines and methods, which impoverish the soul, we must continually point out that human inwardness is a polyphony in which no voice can be 'reduced' to another, and in which the unity cannot be grasped analytically,

but only heard in the present harmony. One of the leading
voices is the instinct of origination.'[6]

Buber goes on to point out that the originator, the creator, is
by nature and necessity solitary, and that he must reach out to
his fellow-creatures lost in the world, to be his friends or comrades beyond the arts. Only in this way does he have an awareness and a share of mutuality. From this point Buber develops his
philosophy of dialogue—dialogue as a principle or method of
education. That does not concern us in the present context—
only his perception that origination is an autonomous instinct, a
solitary activity. I do not wish to claim Buber's authority for the
conclusions I deduce from this fact.

Nevertheless it follows, from the whole philosophy of art
associated with the names I have mentioned, that in the act of
origination, when the artist becomes aware of the instant self,
the fruitful zero of consciousness, he cannot attend to external
injunctions of morality or social propriety. But if we make ourselves free from social responsibility (as we must) we do not
necessarily free ourselves from personal responsibility. 'As we
"become free",' Buber says, 'this leaning on something (a traditional bond, a law, a direction) is more and more denied to us,
and our responsibility must become personal and solitary.'[7]

But must. There can be no origination, no art, no mediation
with the collective unconscious, if we willingly and consciously
submit our instinct of origination to traditional bonds and moral
codes. This is at once the paradox and the dilemma of the situation, and the reason why we must passionately reject all forms
of censorship and legislative control. The artist must be free. But
he must also be responsible.

What is meant by personal responsibility in this context?
In Buber's opinion it presupposes 'one who addresses me

[6] *Between Man and Man.* London, 1947, pp. 85–6.
[7] Ibid., pp. 92–3.

primarily from a realm independent of myself, and to whom I am answerable'. In one word, God. Or we might say Truth—equally an abstraction so far as I am concerned. If I must choose an abstraction, I should say Beauty—the beautiful of the prayer of Socrates: 'grant me to be beautiful in the inner man'. And since we are discussing this question of personal responsibility in relation to literature and the arts, that choice should be adequate. The reason why the genuine artist, the originator, does not usually resort to pornography is because it offends his sense of beauty. I think he sometimes, and legitimately, commits such an offence from a sense of personal responsibility to that other abstraction which we call Truth. That, I am sure, is the justification for Lawrence's offence, and perhaps for Joyce's. But the personal responsibility of the artist in this dilemma must be granted; he must be free to choose between Truth and Beauty, between realism and idealism.

In any whole society the choice should be made without fear of pathological repercussions within the body of society. But modern society is sick, disgustingly sick, and as I have already said, pornography is but one of the symptoms. As Buber says truly, there has never been such a deep-reaching and comprehensive crisis in history as ours, for it is a crisis of confidence in life itself. 'Where confidence reigns man must often, indeed, adapt his wishes to the commands of his community (by which Buber means repression and sublimation of the instincts); but he must not repress them to such an extent that the repression acquires a dominating significance for his life . . . Only if the organic community disintegrates from within and mistrust becomes life's basic note does the repression acquire its dominating importance.' It is in such a condition (which is ours) that sublimation acquires an exceptional importance, for there is no longer a sense of community, 'a human wholeness with the force and the courage to manifest itself. For spirit to arise the energy of the repressed instincts must mostly first be "sublimated", the traces of its origin cling to the spirit and it can mostly assert itself against the instincts only by convulsive alienation. The divorce between spirit and instincts is here, as often, the consequence of the divorce between man and man.'

Another way of saying this would be that an insecure and alienated society has lost the moral right to interfere in affairs of the spirit, and artistic creation, even at the low levels of contemporary fiction, is an affair of the spirit. Pornography does matter, because it is one of the many manifestations of man's spiritual corruption and social alienation; but to treat it as an isolated phenomenon is not merely useless, but positively harmful to the spirit of man, already alienated and sinking in the tumult of our social conflicts. What does not matter is whether *Lady Chatterley's Lover* or *Ulysses* is pornographic in the meaning of the law. The only question is whether such works send out any flicker of light from the sinking lamp of the spirit, and of this there is no question. In all the turbid chaos of modern literature Joyce and Lawrence are among the few authors who give us the conviction that the Spirit of God is still manifest in the creative genius of man, still brooding on the face of the waters.

13

CIVILIZATION AND THE SENSE OF QUALITY

> It is art that makes life, makes interest, makes importance, for
> our consideration and application of these things, and I know
> of no substitute whatever for the force and beauty of its
> process.
>
> Henry James, *Letters*, II, 508.

Art, as I have so often insisted in these pages, is one of those
vague spheres of human activity which escape any very precise
definition. Criticism is merely an approximation towards that
unattainable end, an endless multiplication of distinctions. One
such distinction more firmly established than most is that
between *art* and *entertainment*. An entertainment is something
which distracts us or diverts us from the routine of daily life. It
makes us for the time being forget our cares and worries; it
interrupts our conscious thoughts and habits, rests our nerves
and minds, though it may incidentally exhaust our bodies. Art,
on the other hand, though it may divert us from the normal
routine of our existence, causes us in some way or other to

become conscious of that existence. Matthew Arnold defined poetry as the criticism of life—with a saving clause, if I remember rightly, about 'high seriousness'. I do not like the phrase, for it suggests that art is some kind of intellectual activity. Art is rather an expression of our deepest instincts and emotions; it is a serious activity whose end is not so much to divert as to vitalize. I avoid words like 'improve' and 'uplift' because they only apply to a special kind of art. Art is not necessarily a moral activity, and its tonic effect is made through the senses. Nevertheless, even in its purest, or most abstract—in Oscar Wilde's sense, its most *useless* forms: in one of Shakespeare's songs, or a minuet by Mozart, or a drawing by Boucher—even then art is radically different from amusement. It does not leave us without affecting us, and affecting us, according to some scale of value, for the better.

This virtue in art is shown by its survival value. Historically speaking, we cannot distinguish a civilization except by its art. At any rate, the more a civilization is subjected to the test of time, the more it is reduced to its works of art. The rest rots away. Even the remote periods of pre-history become vivid for a moment in some cave-drawing or fragment of carved bone. Historical civilization begins with the epic poems Gilgamesh, or the Bible, or Homer. Shards of pottery, painted or incised, are more eloquent than the names of emperors or fields of battle. Cities and fertile lands disappear, but buried in their ruins, in tombs and sanctuaries, we find a vase, a jewel, a few coins, made by the artists of those days, which speak to us in clear language and tell us of the status and character of that lost civilization. They tell us not merely that such and such a people worshipped the sun, or that they fought in chariots, or believed in the resurrection of the dead. These are incidental items of knowledge which we might possibly derive from some other source. But works of art speak more directly to us: for by their form and style they give us a measure of the refinement of a civilization. The aesthetic sense—

the faculty by which we appreciate works of art—has its vagaries; at one moment we execrate, say, Gothic architecture, and a century later it is exalted above all other styles. But there is an ideal aesthetic scale of values, just as there is an ideal scale of moral values; and by the measure of this scale all civilizations are given their due rank.

The survival value of art may be readily admitted, but what, the cynic might ask, is the value of survival? What does it matter, what did it matter to the caveman of the Stone Age, or the sculptors of Assyria, or the potters of China, that some remote civilization would disinter their works and judge them good?

Here we face a problem which is fundamental to our faith in the future. It is a fundamental question that divides mankind into those who believe all human activity to be vain, leading to no realizable improvement in this world; and those who believe that man has acquired, however slowly and however tentatively, the instruments of self-improvement, and moves towards a more enjoyable life.

There is a phrase, the perfectibility of man (probably first used by Godwin or his disciple Shelley) which has been the object of much ridicule on the part of those who despair of mankind, and find perfectibility only in divine or unattainable realms of being. It is, obviously, an incautious phrase; a state of perfectibility would be a state of immobility, of final attainment; and it is difficult to conceive of life as thus stabilized. But the phrase does not represent the true doctrine of progress, which is not so much a doctrine as a myth. One can take a long view or a short view of the future of mankind. On a short view we can only be practical and realistic: if man improves, it is at a rate to which we cannot accommodate our immediate politics. A precise set of dogmas is probably as much as one generation can cope with. But a belief in progress belongs to a long view of mankind's future: it is a mythical conception quite parallel to the mythical conceptions of religion. It merely substitutes, for a supernatural Kingdom of Heaven to be attained in another world, a Golden Age to be attained in this world. And as a myth it is as good as any other myth; I would claim that it is much more sensible because it is much more human. The dogma of original sin, which is offered as an alternative, would be insupportable did it not have, as a corollary, the promise of salvation through divine intervention; and one may suggest without cynicism that in this case the wish is father to the thought. The myth of progress, on the other hand, has no illegitimate offspring. It is born as a wish, or as a will, and there is no attempt to disguise its innocent and hopeful nature.

The spirit of disillusionment which prevails in our war-ridden world is probably a reaction to the evolutionary optimism of the nineteenth century. Let us freely admit that much that goes by the name of liberalism is to be identified with that same spirit of optimism. But I think by now we have learned to distinguish between the freedom to do as we like and the duty to create a free world. I see no reason at all why the right to create an artificial scarcity of goods, or the right to exploit native labour in the colonies, should be even remotely associated with the concept of liberty. Liberty and freedom, these values we are now defending, have no economic purpose: they are spiritual values, and as such depend on the fine perceptions of those who guard them. Just as the dogmas of religion depend for their interpretation on fallible human agents, so the ideals of liberty are subject to the same chance. You cannot put on one side certain ideals of life, of conduct, of social order, and say that these represent a divine dispensation to which all men must submit; and on the other side place all other ideals and condemn them as human, all too human. The choice is between the interpretation of dogma, supernatural or divine in origin, and the interpretation of the natural phenomena of life—between faith and reason. In either case the interpreting agent is a human being, and the fallibility inherent in our humanity extends to every range of thought and feeling.

We may therefore reaffirm a rational faith in human progress. But let us be very clear that we do not confuse spiritual with material progress; let us recognize the uncertainty of our aims and the feebleness of our agents; let us proceed with humility and measure. But let us at the same time declare, that throughout all the chances of history, in the face of defeat and despair, in spite of long epochs of darkness and retrogression, man has established faculties that enable him to distinguish between immediate satisfactions and absolute values. He has established a moral sense to guide him in his dealings with his fellow-men and an aesthetic sense to enable him to modify the life of reason; and though the life of reason is still subject to all manner of raids and rebuffs, it exists as a practical ideal, extending to wider and wider circles of humanity, and promising an earthly paradise never to be attained only because each stage towards its realization creates a superior level.

I have just defined the aesthetic sense as the faculty that enables man to modify the quality of his environment. Quality is, of course, the essential word in this definition. There are other faculties, faculties which might be described as technical or practical, that enable man to modify the quantity of his environment: to produce more corn, to utilize more power, to conserve more energy. But these faculties, though they play an important part in the growth of civilization, are not our present concern. I freely admit that in some cases it is difficult to disentangle the two elements: the aesthetic appeal of the Gothic cathedral, for example, depends very directly on the solution of technical problems in building; more obviously, the quality of music has, within certain limits, been governed by the technical perfection of the instruments available.

If we make this distinction between art and the instruments of art, then I think we are bound to admit that whatever progress in art is discernible within historical times is due to an improvement in its instrument rather than to any change in the instinct that operates them. The difference between a bushman's engraving of an antelope and the drawing of a similar animal by Pisanello is fully explained by the difference between a sharpened flint working on the surface of a rock and a silver-point pencil working on parchment. The civilizations behind these two manifestations of the aesthetic sense bear no comparison; but the aesthetic sense is the same. Similarly, who would be bold enough to say that the poetry of Tennyson, or even of Shakespeare, showed any qualitative advance on the poetry of Homer? Whatever art we examine, we are driven to this conclusion: that the underlying faculty or impulse is relatively constant; that the variations are due to the accidents of time and circumstance which release this impulse or faculty. The faculty with which we are endowed must be educated, encouraged, provided with suitable instruments and a rewarding material. Art does not, like technical skill, arise from the necessities of a situation: it is not an invention. Alas, it is perfectly possible for the whole process of civilization to carry on without art. 'To carry on'—the phrase has a provisional ring; and from a wider point of view it is equally certain that a civilization without art will perish—perish materially and fade from the memory of mankind.

Art is grace, art is form, art is—among all possible manners of doing or making a thing—the most memorable. That particular manner of doing or making a thing is memorable because it stimulates our senses, because it brings human inventions within measurable distance of organic growth, because for a moment the will of man seems to be identified with the universal forces of life.

Art redeems our actions from monotony and our minds from boredom. We have to make things and to do things in order to live, but the routine of this endless repetition of menial tasks would dull the senses and deaden the mind unless there was the possibility of doing things and making things with a progressive sense of quality. That sense of quality is the aesthetic sense, and in the end the aesthetic sense is the vital sense, the sense without which we die.

14

THE GREAT DEBATE

Sir Charles Snow's Rede Lecture[1] was a significant contribution to what is undoubtedly the Great Debate of our age: a debate between two philosophies of life which he sees as a 'polarity' of art and science: 'literary intellectuals at one pole—at the other scientists, and as the most representative, the physical scientists'.

Polarity implies an opposition of two, and of only two, possible points of view. That a polarity exists is not to be denied, but to put literary intellectuals at one end of it and physical scientists at the other end is to misrepresent the situation. The title of Sir Charles's lecture is 'The Two Cultures and The Scientific Revolution'; but in fact there are three cultures and the revolution in question is not scientific but technological. Sir Charles confuses the issue by not clearly distinguishing the scientific from the industrial revolutions, for there is a distinction that is both factual and historical. Sir Charles nowhere makes this distinction, and so fails to appreciate the point of view of the 'literary intellectual' (the phrase itself is loaded with prejudice: the critics

[1] *The Two Cultures and the Scientific Revolution*. Cambridge University Press, 1960.

of our technological civilization include, not only poets, but philosophers, politicians, and even men of science like Einstein and Niels Bohr). I do not believe that the typical intellectual is anti-scientific, or ignorant of the elements of science. But he does look with suspicion on technology, which might be defined as the exploitation of scientific knowledge for material gain. The intellectual's case against the Technological Revolution rests on the belief that its processes, which are functional or mechanical, will end by destroying certain mental processes upon which human life, in any valuable sense, finally depends.

It is, fundamentally, a question of values. Science is often defined as the disinterested pursuit of knowledge, that is to say, the accumulation of objective facts. But facts in themselves are valuable only in so far as they serve human ends. It is the ambition of the 'pure' scientist to exclude value-judgements, and that is probably why he now finds himself committed to the Technological Revolution. Technologists do have a system of values; it is perfectly expressed in the adage 'knowledge is power'. Often the aim seems to be power for its own sake, but an ideologist like Sir Charles would probably say that it is power for the sake of productivity, that is to say, for the sake of more goods and a higher standard of living. The intellectual would reply that a higher standard of material comfort is illusory if it can only be secured by functional or mechanical processes that destroy such vital factors as sensuous discrimination and formative imagination. The intellectual's case against the scientist is that he gives his indiscriminate support to technology; his case against technology is that it destroys (perhaps by atrophy rather than by misuse) the vital sources of our humanism.

The scientists have on their side of the Great Debate what they would call 'all the facts'. These facts vary from the starving millions of Asia and Africa, who can only be given a civilized standard of living by an enormously accelerated development of industry and technology, to the dangers of communism, which, according to our politicians, can only be avoided by bigger and better atomic weapons, which only scientists can produce. Our very existence as a nation, Sir Charles warns us, depends on a reorientation of our whole cultural tradition towards science and away from an irrelevant intellectualism.

Sir Charles Snow can hardly disguise his contempt for our leading intellectuals. He mentions Mr. T. S. Eliot, Yeats, Pound and Wyndham Lewis; and though he covers his own opinions by quoting the opinion of an anonymous 'scientist of distinction', or 'most of my scientific acquaintances', or 'non-scientists of strong down-to-earth interest', there can be no doubt that he too shares their low opinion of intellectuals as such. With Plumb and Bullock 'and some of my American sociological friends', he would 'vigorously refuse to be corralled in a cultural box with people they wouldn't be seen dead with, or to be regarded as helping to produce a climate which would not permit of social hope'.

'Nine out of ten of those who have dominated literary sensitivity in our time—weren't they not only politically silly, but politically wicked? Didn't the influence of all they represent bring Auschwitz that much nearer?' Sir Charles agrees—'It is no use denying the facts, which are broadly true. The honest answer was that there is, in fact, a connection, which literary persons were culpably slow to see, between some kinds of early twentieth-century art and the most imbecile expresssions of anti-social feeling. That was one reason among many, why some of us turned our backs on the art and tried to hack out a new and different way for ourselves.'

It might have been more honest of Sir Charles to say that he turned his back on the poetry of Yeats, Pound and Eliot, because he found he had neither the talent nor the taste for it, and that the new or different way he 'hacked out' was both easier and more popular than theirs. But let us ignore that personal aspect of the question: the general accusation is more important.

I have no desire to defend all the political opinions of Yeats, Eliot, Pound or Lewis—on the contrary, I have often in the past expressed my disagreement with them, especially on the question of political means. But in so far as any or all of these writers attacked the prevailing money system (a medieval set-up to which Sir Charles's scientific friends might turn their attention—apart from the Marxists, Soddy is the only distinguished scientist who ever gave it a thought), I fail to see in what respect they were either imbecile or anti-social. It is still possible to maintain, with reason and scientific proof, that usury has been one of the major causes of misery in the modern world, and for wickedness one cannot suggest a rival to those financial and technological monopolies that profit from war and the preparations for war.

There is a science called economics or political economy. It is the disgrace of a technological civilization. It has failed to produce any coherent science of the production, distribution and consumption of the commodities proliferated by machine production. It has failed to give us an international medium of exchange exempt from the fluctuations and disasters of the gold standard. It is split into a riot of rival sects and irreconcilable dogmas which can only be compared to the scholastic bickerings of the Middle Ages. Intellectuals might have more respect for science if in this one most vital subject it would achieve order and enlightenment. It cannot do so, perhaps, because a technological civilization can conceive no controlling ideal other than the materialistic one of a higher standard of living. Standards (as opposed to values) are scientific—they can be measured.

The materialistic standard is not questioned by the scientist, and it is very difficult to criticize it, especially if one is oneself enjoying a high standard of living. Most of our fellow human beings, as Sir Charles points out, are underfed and die before their time, and a 'moral trap' is involved 'which comes through the insight into man's loneliness: it tempts one to sit back, complacent in one's unique tragedy, and let others go without a meal'. As a group, Sir Charles claims, scientists fall into that trap less easily than others: they think that something can be done. They are even optimistic—'tough and good and determined to fight it out at the side of their brother men'. Yes, one knows the type, and that is why so many of them become, and even remain, communists. But (and this is the intellectual counter-attack) they never stop to consider the secondary consequences of the scientific means they would adopt. Sir Charles himself quite complacently (no, hopefully) looks forward to the industrialization of all those areas of the world that are backward in the technological race—India, China, Africa. Only by ruthless, urgent, massive industrialization can the native's mud-hut become an air-conditioned apartment, his daily bowl of rice a succulent steak, his loincloth a decent two-piece Terylene suit, his spinning-wheel an automatic machine. That he will exchange the peace and poverty, the languor and cow-dung of his present village for the noise and lethal fumes of internal-combustion engines, the nervous anxiety and stomach ulcers of the industrialized city, is possibly regarded by Sir Charles as a small price to pay for the material progress he has achieved. He has lost his primitive faith and has no explanation, mythical or religious, for the frantic life he leads; he is the victim of unconscious fears and psychic illnesses, but in compensation he has a longer expectation of life—of a life that is in fact a social neurosis, more wide-spread and devastating than any plague of the past.

I am, presumably, what Sir Charles calls 'an intellectual Luddite'. With Ruskin and Morris, Thoreau, Emerson and Lawrence and other 'men of feeling' for whom he has nothing but contempt, I believe that the technological revolution is a disaster that is likely to end in the extermination of humanity, and I have what I would call scientific reasons for this belief. Life—the vital source of the will to live—depends not on comfort or even on 'health, food and education'. It depends on the free exercise of various innate human faculties—the faculty of perception, for example. Sir Russell Brain, who is a great scientist, has suggested that 'either images or symbols or both combined give us a knowledge of the nature of things beyond both our immediate experiences and the structure of the physical world revealed by science'. This means that science itself, no less than art, depends on the preservation in all its acuteness and awareness of a faculty (the creative imagination) which is destined to die of disuse in a mechanized civilization.

I do not point to this scientific fact for the purpose of undermining science. On the contrary, I am suggesting that there exists in the whole process of industrialization and technological invention a tendency to destroy sensuous perception and imaginative experience, the very faculties upon which our scientific knowledge of the nature of things finally depends. In short, technology (and the automatism that goes with it) tend to destroy human sensibility, and it is upon human sensibility that what is human in us survives. Without sensibility we become robots, that is to say, functional animals incapable of moral and aesthetic responses. Sir Charles nowhere meets the intellectual Luddite's main charge: that the technological revolution lacks any moral or aesthetic foundation, and that nothing pertaining to its structure and procedures can prevent the use of its inventions for anti-vital and inhuman ends. Sir Charles may protest that art and morality are not scientific subjects; if he does he has provided the only evidence of the inhumanity of science that we need. Our complaint about the Scientific Revolution, therefore, is that it is not scientific enough—that it ignores, with fatal consequences for the welfare of humanity, the psyche of man— the neural reflexes by which he functions as something more than animal.

It may seem a paradoxical conclusion but it is the inevitable one: the modern scientific ideologist (for Sir Charles himself does not claim to be a scientist) is superficial. It is not only that he can utter a 'straightforward truth' such as 'Industrialization is the only hope of the poor' without any sense of its crookedness; it is rather that he can accept a revolution, 'the Scientific Revolution', for its material benefits without for a moment considering the cost in human values.

Sir Charles may protest that he uses the word 'hope in a crude and prosaic' sense, and he says he has 'not much use for the moral sensibility of anyone who is too refined to use it'. Is a moral sensibility too refined if it sees through the deceptions of those who export sewing-machines and syphilis (or to be more up to date, tractors and cancer of the lung) and call it civilization? Intellectuals like Albert Schweitzer and Carlo Dolci do not cry out for the industrialization of the poor communities in which they live and work—they ask for land and for the tools with which to cultivate it.

Admittedly we shall need science to preserve human values; the hungry multitudes proliferate, and they can only be fed by scientific methods of agriculture. And only science can prevent them proliferating. Food production and contraception—if only science could concentrate on these two problems, to the neglect of atomic power and journeys to the moon! Sir Charles might argue that there is no distinction; in a scientific age the way to plenty winds round the moon. But that is to make the ends justify the means, a moral obtuseness that seems to be inseparable from the scientific mind.

I will not speak of a tragic sense of life, which in the past has been the source of moral dignity—are we not all agreed that tragedy is to be banished from the Welfare World? But a sense of greatness—that is perhaps optimistic enough for the scientist to accept as an ideal. But does he realize with Burckhardt, that even this ideal 'resides in the power to forgo benefits in the name of morality, in voluntary self-denial, not merely from motives of prudence but from goodness of heart'?

15

THE ARTS AND PEACE

> The task of art is enormous. Through the influence of real art, aided by science, guided by religion, that peaceful co-operation of man which is now maintained by external means—by our law-courts, police, charitable institutions, factory inspection, and so forth—should be obtained by man's free and joyous activity. Art should cause violence to be set aside.
>
> And it is only art that can accomplish this.
>
> Leo Tolstoy.

These words of deep conviction come at the conclusion of *What is Art?*, Tolstoy's last great polemical work.[1] Tolstoy was convinced that an intimate relationship exists between the structure of society and art, and he came to this conviction because he realized that art is a biological process ('an organ of human life') the function of which is to 'transmit reasonable perception into feeling'. Reasonable perception, by which he meant a combin-

---

[1] *What is Art? and Essays on Art*. Trans. Aylmer Maude. Oxford University Press, 1930.

ation of the faculties of science and religion, could free mankind from illusions (religious, social or judicial), establish the brotherhood of man as the only reasonable ideal, and art would then present this ideal in moving and persuasive forms. All arts are arts of persuasion: by creating images, symbols, fables, they can diffuse throughout the community the best that is thought and felt 'by the best members of society'. In a simile of utmost naïvety Tolstoy ends his essay on *What is Art?* with the suggestion that the religious art of the future 'will lay in the souls of men the rails along which the actions of those whom art thus educates will naturally pass'.

The method recommended by Tolstoy has a suspicious resemblance to the practices of the modern advertiser: art is the hidden persuader. If peace is what you want, they might say, then give us the money and in next to no time there will be a universal demand for it. Brotherly union among men is, indeed, the declared ideal of certain religious or ethical organizations which do not hesitate to make use of the wiles of the advertiser.

We know instinctively that Tolstoy was mistaken—not in his ideals, and not in his insights, but in his theories and definitions. His definition of art is a definition of one kind of art—the kind which, on an earlier page, I have called 'realism'. Art can equally well begin with feeling and seek perceptual images to express such feelings—the kind of art I have called 'expressionism'. As for science, Tolstoy admits that hitherto it has deviated from its true purpose (which should be 'to demonstrate the irrationality, unprofitableness and immorality, of war and executions; or the inhumanity and harmfulness of prostitution; or the absurdity, harmfulness, and immorality of using narcotics or eating animals; of the irrationality, harmfulness and obsolescence of patriotism'). But Tolstoy nowhere explains how the purpose of science is to be changed from 'producing articles of luxury or weapons of man-destroying war' to its true purpose. His whole argument is a vicious circle: for art can only cause violence to be set aside if it is motivated by a science transformed by ethical or religious ideals. All depends on the prevalence of 'a common religious perception', which is precisely what the modern world lacks.

And yet the root of the matter is in Tolstoy, not so much in his polemical essays, as in his works of imagination. Tolstoy realized that there is a subtle but mysterious connection between art and violence: that they are dialectical opposites and that art and only art can eliminate violence from the heart of man.

How does art operate on the heart of man—or on his mind? The answer to this question was first given by Plato. All the arts, his argument ran, are essentially harmonic—they make their effect by rhythm, physical waves that beat on the confused senses and induce a feeling of eudemony or well-being. Plato antici-pated Pavlov in a theory of conditioned reflexes. He gave priority among the arts to group activities, choric songs and dances, and in The Laws he defined a well-educated man as one who could sing and dance well. Education, he said, is 'learning to feel pleas-ure and pain about the right things' (a definition to which Aristotle gave his unqualified approval) and in all seriousness he asserted that 'the whole aesthetic and moral training of the child can be brought under the heading of education in the "choric art", the art of song accompanied by the strains of the lyre and the movements of an appropriate ballet d'action' (A. E. Taylor's gloss in his Introduction to The Laws).[2] All the arts are forms of physical drill, but the drill is based on true canons of taste in music, on correct harmonics. If peace is your aim, then there is a harmony which will inculcate it infallibly. But if war is your aim, you must change the music.

This is a perfectly reasonable and coherent theory. Unfortunately it has never been put to the test on a nation-wide scale. The objection that if it were true we should find all people who have been trained in choral music and dance exceptionally

[2] The Laws of Plato. Trans. by A. E. Taylor. London (Dent), 1934.

pacific in temperament, whereas they are as subject as other people to irrational passions, may or may not be a correct generalization, but it is irrelevant to Plato's argument, which demands uniformity and universality of action. Plato was always insisting on the profound effects of environment; we are worked upon by what we see as well as by what we hear and how we move. Choric dances in an ugly environment might mitigate the bad effects of such visual misproportions; it would not prevent them. For this reason education must always be total. A well-trained élite might set a good example (which is really what Tolstoy also envisaged), but essential to Plato's theory is the belief that ideas do not change men; they are changed by physical forces only. The mind is a malleable substance, ready to be impressed for good or evil by whatever it receives through the senses. It should be overwhelmed with harmonic sights and sounds, proceeding from every quarter, 'like a breeze bearing health from happy regions', so that 'some influence from noble works constantly falls upon eye and ear from childhood upward, and imperceptibly draws them into sympathy and harmony with the beauty of reason, whose impress they take'. And it is in the Republic, from which this passage comes, that Plato also makes clear the communal basis of his aim. The purpose of it all is not 'to make one class specially happy, but to ensure the welfare of the commonwealth as a whole. By persuasion or constraint it will unite the citizens in harmony, making them share whatever benefits each class can contribute to the common good; and its purpose in forming men of that spirit was not that each should be left to go his own way, but that they should be instrumental in binding the community into one.'

It may seem a long cry from the ideal republic of Plato to the realities of a world rent by political passions and living under the immediate threat of universal extermination by atomic warfare. What is the purpose of the arts in such a world? We can only affirm that the purpose is the same today as it was in the war-ridden world of Plato; and I know of no other remedy for our condition half so realistic as the education through art recommended by Plato. Men's minds must be changed; that must be the single and insistent aim of all our policies if we are to avoid mutual destruction. How is it possible to change men's minds?—that is the only worthwhile question. But to change them not for the moment or for an immediate advantage: to change them permanently and universally. That is the question; and the only answer we receive at present is that men's minds can and must be changed by moral suasion. I believe this is an illusion.

What is morality? It is not a state of mind but a mode of action. Our morals are not defined by what we believe but by what we do. The root is the Latin *mos* (pl. *mores*) and it meant originally a way of carrying oneself, physical uprightness, traditional behaviour. Mores were transmitted by custom, by the imitation of parents and teachers, and there was always present a sense of personal responsibility for one's actions. Impossible to trace here the steps by which such *habits of perfection* became codified and generalized into abstractions, into *laws of conduct* to which conscious compliance was exacted—an unreal relationship. The consequence was a weakening of the bonds of traditional behaviour. If man is no longer responsible to himself, but to an abstraction, he has a thousand chances to be evasive, to be weak, to be mistaken. If he acts, no longer instinctively and automatically, but by calculation and with circumspection, he tends to act ambiguously and intolerantly.

The true sense of morals was lost among the philosophers and theologians, but it is being regained by the writers of today, especially in France, which has always been a country concerned with moral conduct rather than moral codes—one has only to recall Montaigne, Rochefoucauld, Vauvenargues. This realism reappears in the deeply perceptive works of Saint-Exupéry and Camus—even in Malraux, to whom art is above all transforming action. Saint-Exupéry is perhaps the writer who has most clearly (certainly most accessibly) expressed a philosophy of moral realism, which perhaps accounts for his enormous influence on the post-war generation in France (and his failure to make a like impression on the flabby moral tissue of the post-war generation in Great Britain and the United States). 'To be human is precisely to be responsible—responsible a little for the destiny of mankind, in the measure of his work.' Saint-Exupéry (in Terre des Hommes) is referring to practical work, to group responsibility, to the fraternity of action—not a responsibility to moral absolutes, but to our neighbours, Tolstoy's brotherhood of man. There are no systems of right action, but only an instinctive uprightness, a good, because free and unselfish, behaviour.

'The work of Saint-Exupéry is not an argument,' writes one of his best commentators.[3] 'It is an example.' Thus we return to Plato—at least, to the idea that art can have a moral effect, as action and not as persuasion. Gide once remarked that Saint-Exupéry's great discovery was that man's happiness lies not in freedom but in his acceptance of a duty. Substitute destiny or necessity for duty and Gide's observation is a commonplace of Greek philosophy. Saint-Exupéry is saying something more original than this, something more pertinent to our contemporary dilemma. He is saying that the one thing that matters is the effect of action, of the constructive, the creative effort. 'Constrain them to join in building a tower,' says the desert prince to his son in Citadelle (The Wisdom of the Sands),[4] and you shall make them like brothers. But if you would have them hate each other, throw food amongst them. A civilization is built on what is required of men, not on that which is provided for them. . . . Man is, above

[3] Everett W. Knight, Literature Considered as Philosophy (Routledge & Kegan Paul), 1957.

[4] The Wisdom of the Sands, by Antoine de Saint-Exupéry. Trans. by Stuart Gilbert. London (Hollis & Carter), 1952.

all, he who creates. And theirs alone is brotherhood who work together.'

This is a better recipe for peace than Tolstoy's muddled talk of perception and feeling, because art is conceived as action that transforms man, and neither the intelligence of science nor 'reasonable religious perception' is a pre-requisite for its beneficent effect. One of the many fables in *The Wisdom of the Sands* is about two gardeners who had lived and worked together for many years and were then separated, to their great distress. After many years one of the gardeners received a letter from his friend. Full of delight and anticipating detailed news of his friend's adventures, he brought the letter to the prince and begged him to read it, 'as one begs a friend to read a poem'. The prince opened the letter and read: *This morning I pruned my rose trees*—and that was all. A great change befell the gardener: his peace of mind was gone; but it was not until three years later that he had a chance to reply to his friend's letter. 'From now on he took to spending whole days in his room, jotting down phrases, crossing them out, starting again, sticking out his tongue the while, like a schoolboy poring over his lesson-book. He knew he had something important to say, and somehow he must transport himself . . . to his absent friend. For he had to build a bridge over the sundering gulf and, communing with the friend who was his other self, across Space and Time, make known to him his love. Thus a day came when, blushing, he came to me and showed me his answer, hoping to glimpse on my face a reflection of the joy that would light up that of its recipient, and to test on me the power of his message. And when I read it, I saw these words, written in a careful yet unskilled hand—earnest as a prayer coming from the heart, yet how simple and how humble!—*This morning I, too, pruned my rose trees . . .*'

A simple parable, but it expresses the truth. It may remind us of the conclusion of *Candide*, but Voltaire was more cynical and more resigned. 'Il faut cultiver nos jardins' is a moral command.

Saint-Exupéry means that growing roses is a constructive effort, a work like building a tower, an art; and that so long as men are joined together in creative activities, they will live at peace. The prince in the story fell silent, 'musing on that essential thing I was beginning to perceive more clearly; for it was Thou, O Lord, whom they were honouring, fusing their lives together within Thee, above and beyond their rose trees, *though they knew it not*'.

That is the last but not the least important point to make. Our creative activities should be instinctive, habitual. The artist of today is isolated, alienated from his fellow-men and from nature. The effort he makes is a conscious effort, an assertion of the self, often an angry protest against his impotency. He has this great healing power in his possession, but no one comes to him for help. He cannot act alone, even for his own salvation. His true work is communal. Other artists must be with him, working on the same project. Indeed, all men must be with him, each an artist according to his kind, all men artists participating in the work that has to be done, all work being done as art.

This may be a gentle doctrine to offer amid the tyrannical brutalities of our time, but we are considering the contribution which the arts can make to the cause of peace, and their contribution cannot in the nature of things be immediate. But a beginning can be made, especially among minds not yet hardened by the extremities of strife. No one knows how much grace we are given; but while a grain of hope remains, action is possible; towards unity, towards mutual understanding, towards the reform of education, towards the slow process of learning to work together creatively, whatever this may cost in pride and self-assertiveness.

INDEX

Routledge Classics
Get inside a great mind

The Culture Industry
Selected essays on mass culture
Theodor Adorno

'A volume of Adorno's essays is equivalent to a whole shelf of books on literature.'
Susan Sontag

Adorno's finest essays are collected here, offering the reader unparalleled insights into his thoughts on culture. He argued that the culture industry commodified and standardized all art. In turn this suffocated individuality and destroyed critical thinking. In today's world, where even the least cynical of consumers is aware of the influence of the media, Adorno's work takes on a more immediate significance. *The Culture Industry* is an unrivalled indictment of the banality of mass culture.

Hb: 0–415–25534–1   Pb: 0–415–25380–2

The Stars Down to Earth
and other essays on the irrational in culture
Theodor Adorno

'There can be no question of the contemporary importance and relevance of these essays. Adorno is one of the great critics of the role of irrational authoritarianism in contemporary society.'
Douglas Kellner, author of Media Culture

Presenting four of Adorno's key writings on the irrational in mass culture these essays concentrate on the darker side of the modern and reach some profoundly disquieting conclusions. The author's arguments could easily describe the present age, in which extreme political and religious movements are increasingly commonplace, making Adorno's essays, written fifty years ago, a remarkably prescient and indispensable commentary on our times.

Hb: 0–415–27099–5   Pb: 0–415–27100–2

For these and other classic titles from Routledge, visit
www.routledgeclassics.com

Routledge Classics
Get inside a great mind

The Fear of Freedom
Erich Fromm

'Erich Fromm speaks with wisdom, compassion, learning and insight into the problems of individuals trapped in a social world that is needlessly cruel and hostile.'
Noam Chomsky

Erich Fromm sees right to the heart of our contradictory needs for community and for freedom like no other writer before or since. In *The Fear of Freedom*, Fromm warns that the price of community is indeed high, and it is the individual who pays. He leaves a valuable and original legacy to his readers – a vastly increased understanding of the human character in relation to society.

Hb: 0–415–25542–2   Pb: 0–415–25388–8

The Sane Society
Erich Fromm

'Dr Fromm is deeply concerned with the most important unifying questions that can be asked about contemporary western society – is it sane?'
Asa Briggs

Analysing conformity in contemporary patriarchal and capitalistic societies, this searing critique of the status quo was published to wide acclaim and even wider condemnation. A scathing indictment of modern capitalism by one of the twentieth century's greatest political thinkers, this controversial book is arguably more relevant now than at any other time. Read it and decide for yourself – are *you* living in a sane society?

Pb: 0–415–27098–7

For these and other classic titles from Routledge, visit
www.routledgeclassics.com

Routledge Classics
Get inside a great mind

Marxism and Literary Criticism
Terry Eagleton

'Terry Eagleton is that rare bird among literary critics – a real writer.'
Colin McCabe, The Guardian

A wonderfully clear introduction to the application of Marx's theories to the study of literature. Short and very well-written, it provides a survey of major twentieth-century literary theorists, including Marcuse, Jameson and Lukács. In this ground-breaking work, Eagleton applies viewpoints central to Marxist thought to his analysis. Through this, he is able to show the part that Marxist criticism has to play in defining the crucial link between literature and historical condition.

Hb: 0–415–28583–6   Pb: 0–415–28584–4

The Political Unconscious
Narrative as a socially symbolic act
Fredric Jameson

'Fredric Jameson is generally considered to be one of the foremost contemporary English-language Marxist literary and cultural critics.'
Douglas Kellner

In this ground-breaking and influential study Fredric Jameson explores the complex place and function of literature within culture. At the time Jameson was actually writing the book, in the mid- to late seventies, there was a major reaction against deconstruction and post-structuralism. As one of the most significant literary theorists of the time, Jameson found himself in the unenviable position of wanting to defend his intellectual past yet keep an eye on the future. With this book he carried it off beautifully.

Hb: 0–415–28750–2   Pb: 0–415–28751–0

For these and other classic titles from Routledge, visit
www.routledgeclassics.com

Routledge Classics
Get inside a great mind

Language of Fiction
Essays in criticism and verbal analysis of the English novel
David Lodge

'Something of a milestone in English criticism. . . . an important addition to English critical writing about the genre of the novel.'
Tony Tanner, The Modern Language Review

Language of Fiction was the first book of criticism by the renowned novelist and critic David Lodge. In it, he established a fresh approach to the appreciation of literature that focuses the reader's attention on the significance of language. This major work, from the pen of one of England's finest living writers, is essential reading for all those who care about the creation and appreciation of literature.

Hb: 0–415–29002–3   Pb: 0–415–29003–1

Romantic Image
Frank Kermode

'In this extremely important book of speculative and scholarly criticism Mr Kermode is setting out to redefine the notion of the Romantic tradition, especially in relation to English poetry and criticism . . . a rich, packed, suggestive book.'
Times Literary Supplement

One of our most brilliant and accomplished critics, Frank Kermode here redefines our conception of the Romantic movement, questioning both society's harsh perception of the artist as well as poking fun at the artist's occasionally inflated self-image. Written with characteristic wit and style, this ingeniously argued and hugely enjoyable book is a classic of its kind.

Hb: 0–415–26186–4   Pb: 0–415–26187–2

For these and other classic titles from Routledge, visit
www.routledgeclassics.com

Routledge Classics
Get inside a great mind

Printed in the United States
by Baker & Taylor Publisher Services